# REBOOT

*After* Recovery from Trauma

# REBOOT

*After* Recovery from Trauma

## LIFE HACKS

### TO OVERCOME POST-TRAUMA FATIGUE & PARALYSIS

Bonnie Zieman

ISBN

Cover design by Bonnie Zieman

To everyone looking to get unstuck and move forward with life.

"Every moment is a fresh beginning."

-T.S. Eliot

# CONTENTS

# 1. REBOOT OVERVIEW

Reboot definition: *"to shut down and restart; to start anew; make a new start or create a new version."* Merriam Webster

S O, YOU THINK you need a reboot. Everyone has experienced the need for a psychological reboot at some point in their life. Perceiving oneself as stuck, stalled, or unable to move forward with life often occurs when one also feels disconnected, over-burdened, confused, powerless, fatigued, fearful, or lacking purpose. While the information provided in this book can help anyone who feels stalled, this reboot assistance is particularly for people who feel stuck after recovering from trauma due to being caught in, leaving, and then recovering from an abusive high-control experience or group.

Your experience of feeling stuck in your movement forward with life after recovering from being deceived, manipulated, exploited and/or abused will have its own unique source, trajectory, and meaning. Among many possibilities, it may be that:

- you now find yourself at a crossroads
- thwarted dreams are demanding your attention
- due to unexpected reversals you feel you have temporarily lost your way

- you feel you have still not divested yourself of limiting beliefs and behaviors
- important goals and plans have not come to pass.
- an opportunity is beckoning and yet you feel unable to respond
- character traits encouraged by a coercive milieu still hold you back
- you keep looking back, longing for old relationships, rewards or comforts
- you are exhausted after all the hard work of recovery from trauma.

It is possible issues outside of your control play a role in your feeling unable to move forward with life. A physical disability or chronic illness may inhibit your progress forward. Financial issues may impede progress toward your goals. An economic downturn may have set you back. Political turmoil or systemic racial discrimination may make it difficult to envision your path forward. Your own temperament (whether you tend to be pessimistic, prone to anxiety, lack self-esteem, etc.) makes it challenging to leave old patterns and initiate new ones. Issues such as these, however, only make forward movement more challenging, they do not make it impossible.

You may wonder *"How can I 'reboot' during a worldwide pandemic?"* While in years like 2020, you may not be able to activate new strategies out in the world due to government health safety measures, you can embrace the techniques and questions offered here for introspection, inner growth, envisioning dreams, and mapping goals. Profit from extra time you have during lockdowns and/or unexpected downtime to do the inner work that will prime you for reboot work out in the world when the time is right.

As we cope with the storms, fires, floods, viral epidemics, and upheavals caused by climate change, pollution, species extinction and the avarice and corruption of governments around the world, we all have to rethink our values and the way we live our lives. Countries, cities, families, and individuals will have to change their habitual 'operating systems' if they wish to see future generations thrive and the planet survive. The Earth is, perhaps, forcing us all to reconsider and reset our values, priorities and behaviors.

Whether your perception of being stuck is due to a stall in personal/spiritual growth or aspirational achievement, the steps to getting unstuck are basically the same. Life hacks provided in this book will help you re-examine, re-imagine and reboot your life – whatever the source or circumstance of this current feeling of inertia.

As a psychotherapist I occasionally had clients who, after completing therapy, came back saying they felt stalled in their progress forward regardless of the particular issue involved. They often phrased their request for an appointment by saying they wanted to return for a "*tune-up*". With a couple of sessions of reviewing, clarifying, questioning, exploring, and reflecting they soon discovered how they could extricate themselves from the seeming impasse. Many of the strategies, tools and techniques shared in this book are the ones I used to help those clients better understand their perception of being stuck and uncover their path forward.

There is nothing wrong with you if you feel stuck. Being stalled in your movement forward is not a statement about your character, how hard you have worked, nor the value of your plans or projects. Give yourself permission to find yourself in a temporary stall without evaluation or judgment. You have already taken a major step on your path forward by acknowledging you have stalled and reaching for help with this book.

If you have recently exited a controlling group or abusive family system, perhaps you assumed upon leaving that whatever you had internalized of their 'operating system' would no longer be a factor in your life. You may have imagined, that after a period of grieving, the wounds would heal and you would automatically begin afresh.

As you struggle now to survive in a world you have probably been trained to fear and condemn, or as you encounter unforeseen circumstances, you may abandon the work required to move forward. Now that some time has elapsed you may realize you have not entirely flushed your memory of the coercive milieu's 'malware' intrusions. Or, perhaps you have worked so hard to recover from high-control abuse that you are now experiencing recovery fatigue or paralysis.

To a certain degree, our minds function much like a computer. For example, if your mind was saturated with cult indoctrination you were not the one in charge of its programing. Even once out of the group, hidden 'files' may still control your thinking, your perceptions of what is possible, and even habitual 'operating' patterns. You may have left the coercive system but not all of it has left you. Old corrupt files may be lurking within, making you blind or unresponsive to obvious opportunities.

Perhaps you have not yet taken the time to troubleshoot exactly what internal programs are still operating and suppressing natural instincts to move ahead with your life. Perhaps old beliefs are still unconsciously driving your feelings, choices, and actions. Perhaps you are unsure how to restore your authentic self and activate its unique potential. Perhaps you feel stuck in a loop where you stall, restart, and then crash again. This is typical, for example, of anyone who has been indoctrinated into a strict, all-encompassing belief system. The programing runs deep and has been running for a while. Sometimes it takes more than a simple 'refresh' to clear out the malware and begin again with uncorrupted files.

The use here of computer terminology is to illustrate how you need to rout out old files, programs, and operating systems in order to reboot your post-trauma life. In case you need your memory refreshed about exactly what a reboot does for a computing device, here is a list of descriptors that could equally apply to any post-trauma reboot.

*A computer reboot*:

- *Closes all programs*
- *Eliminates residual junk kept in memory*
- *Fixes impaired connections*
- *Restores fast, optimal performance*
- *Can force a temporary shutdown when unresponsive*
- *Erases anything not saved in hard drive*
- *Allows a clean restart*

Such descriptors sound like an apt representation of what trauma survivors need to do with residual programing (junk) that is preventing them from relaunching into life.

Perhaps you assumed you had eliminated all the "residual junk" of the parental or coercive group program but you still have powerful internal images, thought patterns or behaviors that corrupt your ability to proceed smoothly into your new life. Perhaps you are not yet the "sole administrator" of your "operational hard drive". With this reboot intervention we are going to troubleshoot any current operating issues and use some innovative hacks to un-install corrupt files and make sure your new operating system is fully functional, and above all your own.

People get stuck all the time. Those same people also get unstuck. Getting stuck and unstuck is a part of being human. This book and your work in conjunction with it will accelerate your movement out of any stuck pattern in which you find yourself. This impasse will eventually become just another old file in your biographical archives. There are several adjustments and approaches you can take to make that the case.

Some of the scars of control, deception, exploitation and/or abuse can remain sensitive and easily activated by a word, a current event, or a memory. Post recovery from exploitation, unanticipated crises can re-open and re-activate these scars. If that is the case for you

– as it was for me at one point – it can leave you feeling discouraged, disheartened and wondering if you will ever be able to move forward.

In his book, "Getting Unstuck", Timothy Butler tells us when we feel stuck we suffer and invariably feel "... *stale or unchallenged ... agitated, deflated, or downright bored. We are desperate to find a meaningful way to contribute ... to find a reinvigorated role, to dive back into the current of our own lives. We sense that life is flowing all around us, but we sit like a boulder in a river, yearning to be swept along and transformed by the river's great energy.*"

Are you longing to "*find a meaningful way to contribute*" and "*to find a reinvigorated role*" in the current of life, as Butler describes? If so that is good news. If Butler can so precisely describe how anyone can feel stuck, it tells us it is a common human experience. You are not alone. You will feel less alone now that you have this book to help you exit old programs and redesign and reboot your way forward.

After leaving a high-control group or family system you have to grieve the death of a way of life, a belief system, former roles, ways of being, and the loss of friends and family who may decide to reject you when you leave. Perhaps you have to grieve having been deceived and betrayed. You may have to grieve all that was stolen from you in terms of time, energy, and opportunities. If you do not make time to grieve consciously, the grief stores itself in your cells and waits until you are ready. Being weighed down with heavy emotions such as grief makes it difficult to 'adjust settings', install and function from your own operating system and re-embrace life.

Timothy Butler goes on to describe feeling stuck as both an impasse and an opportunity – and even further – a developmental necessity:

"*Faced with a crisis ... we try to push our way forward using our old views and methods. Soon we realize this is not working ... Energy and inspiration begin to evaporate; our conviction seems less certain. We begin to hear the stinging voice of our inner critic and old doubts about our ability ... We seem to be both sinking and moving backward. These feelings at first may bring alarm, but we must come to recognize them as signals that an important process is beginning. Being at impasse is a developmental necessity. It can lead to a new way of understanding and a new type of information.*" Being stuck is a well-known phenomenon and part of what drives personal development.

Experts from a host of fields reveal that human development and growth invariably necessitate overcoming roadblocks, barriers, plateaus, disconfirmations, and setbacks. The good news is feeling stuck is a normal part of the process of change, learning, and human development. Again, do not condemn or criticize yourself for feeling stuck. You need to forgive yourself for any feelings of having reached an impasse so you do not add layers of shame onto feeling stuck.

As a victim of coercive controls who found a way to leave and has endured all the dreadful aftermath of so doing, you have already acquired a wealth of life experience and hard-won understanding. What you already know is waiting to find a venue for expression. Inherent in the act of leaving any control system is a strong desire for self-expression. Even though you feel stuck, your true self is still desirous of self-expression. In fact, your true self has prompted you to find help to get unstuck, seize your right to be, and express who you are now.

With this life reboot book we will work together to access your true self and its inner knowing about exactly what it needs and wants to express. You will also claim, reaffirm and refine knowledge and skills you already possess. You will uncover competencies you need to acquire to move forward. You will find life hacks on how to do all of the above and your own ideas will surely flow as a result of the many creative prompts, strategies, and questions provided.

## USING QUESTIONS TO INITIATE A PSYCHOLOGICAL REBOOT

To effect a reboot from any sense of operational failure, this book provides you with self-searching questions rather than only pages of suggestions. These questions will act as anti-paralysis prompts to help you do the very individual work needed to close the door on your unduly coercive past and to discover what you need now in order to move forward.

The best answers for anyone are always their own. Part of what this book hopes to accomplish is to help you trust your own voice, your own answers – something never encouraged in a high control group. Lao Tzu makes an important point in this regard: *"At the center of your being you have the answer; you know who you are and you know what you want."*

The many lists of introspective questions provided in this book will help you laser in on who you are now, what you value, and what you want. Your answers may surprise and will certainly re-energize you.

Recovery from trauma (physical, emotional, spiritual) is a "process" not a one-time event – nor is a life reboot. A reboot is an active progression or unfolding, not a passive one. It involves many steps. If you are feeling stuck in your recovery from an unduly controlling, traumatic past and the limitations it imposed, it could be due to having stopped the healing work required to recover.

As time passes and life makes it demands, you may occasionally wonder if your recovery from the indoctrination, trauma, or abuse is complete. You will know you are well on the road to recovery from coercive control or exploitation when you find yourself becoming:

- more hopeful
- less pre-occupied with the past
- less caught in a victim mentality
- less caught up in resentment, bitterness, reactivity
- better able to sleep without disturbance
- more engaged with life
- more able to fully and competently attend to your own needs
- better able to regulate your emotions
- less isolated or disconnected
- more able to enjoy meaningful work and relationships
- less fear-based – more love-based
- less governed by demands/expectations of parents, partners, or organizations
- more able to think independently and critically

When feeling stalled, it is helpful to review exactly what you have endured and how you have coped – how you have recovered. Such a review will help you answer the questions of where or how you stalled and provide clues as to what you need to do now to refresh or reboot. James Hollis, psychoanalyst, in his book "*On This Journey We Call Our Life*" says, "*… so must we ask of our lives what task of growth is demanded … we are asked a question by life, and our life is a question. What does it want of us? What is demanded that we may live it more fully?*"

Questions in the next chapter of this book will help you consider if you are still in the crisis/recovery part of leaving the coercive system, which requires time, patience, grief work, and perhaps therapy **or** if you are at the point where you recognize the need to challenge yourself to move out of your comfort zone and do the work needed to reassess, rethink, reimagine, reset, and move ahead into your new life.

In another of James Hollis' books, "*Tracking the Gods*", he asks:

- *"What is your life's vocation or "calling" (as opposed to source of economic livelihood)?*
- *When did your childhood end?*
- *When did you leave home?*
- *Have you left home?*
- *How do your dependencies manifest?*
- *How do you repeatedly hurt yourself, undermine yourself?*
- *Where are you stuck in your journey?*
- *How are you still carrying Mother, Father?*
- *What fears block you?*
- *What is the unlived life that haunts you? …"* (bullet points added)

## RECOVERY or REBOOT?

Crisis management, trauma recovery, and emotional healing require time. If you are still in the middle of the crisis of leaving, recovering from the trauma of being in a coercive control group, dealing with the loss of friends and family, and/or healing the accompanying emotional wounds, this may **not** be the time to consider a life reboot. When in the active process of recovery from trauma you need to allow time to face and express your grief about all the losses. Pressuring yourself to just move past the stage of healing/recovery is counterproductive and the grief will only come back at a later date demanding to be addressed.

Psychological trauma is a distressing experience that overwhelms the brain's ability to cope and that can evoke feelings of helplessness in what can then seem like a hostile world. The brain can heal itself from the debilitating effects of trauma. Healing requires self-care, a sense of physical and emotional safety, time, a period of processing and grieving, and support. Once you have satisfied such healing initiatives you will be ready to consider moving forward with your life.

A life reboot is something you should consider only **after** you have been out of a high-control group for a while and feel you have not moved forward as hoped**.** A life reboot is a process that requires reflection, re-assessment, decision-making, planning, risk-taking, and action rather than active grieving or learning to manage symptoms of post-traumatic stress.

As you work with the questions throughout this book you may discover that you prematurely aborted the grief and emotion-management work and now have to go back and complete it. It is possible to do the recovery work in a short period of time, but if there is deeply buried grief, rage, distrust, etc. due to the complexity of trauma (e.g. sexual abuse) it may take more time and you should postpone a life reboot project such as this for a later date.

The best thing would be to do any grieving work with a licensed therapist. However, if you cannot consider therapy at this time, I have written other books that help with the recovery process in general and recovery from cult exploitation in particular, and would suggest you read them and follow the suggestions that resonate with you.

It is important to offer yourself acceptance and understanding wherever you are in your healing process. You may be expecting too much of yourself in terms of the pace of recovery – especially if:

- due to your exit from a cult you have lost your marriage, home, or children
- you are severely depressed and/or experiencing suicidal ideation
- you are caught in a situation of on-going crisis or domestic abuse
- you have been diagnosed with PTSD or complex PTSD.

If that is the case, you are *not* in a place where you need a life reboot. You first need to work with the ebb and flow of your recovery process, preferably with a mental health professional. You are not stuck. You are in the middle of a complex healing process. Honor it and your unique timing. Come back to this book once you have completed the emotional healing work required.

*However*, if you have determined you are not in the middle of a depressive episode, or suffering from PTSD, or justifiably in the middle of grieving profound losses, then it may be time to consider whether you are simply stalled in your movement toward your new life and are ready for practical life hacks on how to initiate a reboot.

What does it mean to be stalled? You are stalled or stuck if you are feeling: *derailed, demoralized, thwarted, blocked, discouraged, hindered, impeded, obstructed, restrained,* etc.

My experience in a coercive control situation was in a cult as a born-in, third generation member of the Jehovah's Witnesses organization. I will share a few experiences from my time in, and getting out of that high-control group. Although several of the examples in this book of being stuck will reference my time as a member of the Jehovah's Witnesses (aka Watchtower organization or JW dot org) - the information and life hacks here apply equally to:

- people who have left controlling and/or abusive family systems
- the Amish
- Hassidic or Ultra-Orthodox Judaism
- Mormons

- Scientologists

- radical evangelism; etc., etc.

While the specifics of control and manipulation experienced in each system may differ, the *need* to, and the *how* to, remove 'corrupt files' is basically the same.

I hope, therefore, you will adapt what I share about my experiences to your particular high-control group or trauma experience. This book is less about *what* was programed into you than about *how* you can reboot and complete the process of eliminating old, corrupt files — whatever the specific content, whatever the specific source.

In the past few years I received requests to write a book for those who have been out of a cult for several years but still feel they have not done all they can to close the door on the past and to move ahead with life. This book was written partly in response to those articulated needs.

The needs of those who have been free for a while will be different than the needs of someone who has just exited a traumatic situation. This book is designed to help a stall in embracing your new life — at whatever point. It will help you access your inner knowing about what you now need to learn, release, restore, recalibrate, express, and do.

There are over 350 probing questions in this book, similar to what a therapist would pose over months in the consultation room. Such questions would help the client access their own felt sense of what is right for them — their values, desires, and unique way of creating a meaningful life.

Since each person is at a different point in their post-trauma journey, you may find that some of the 350+ questions may not be applicable to your particular situation. Just move on to the next one. The occasional question may seem like a rewording of a previous question, but fresh phrasing can often trigger a new insight.

Most chapters in this book will offer questions to help explore assumptions and beliefs and determine which may be outdated, limiting files from the past. By examining and reassessing your life using questions you will begin constructing a new narrative/script for your life – the ultimate life reboot! I'm excited about the format of this book. It is a jumpstart guide that will allow you to:

- refresh your perspective and re-envision your story
- understand and challenge your fears and habitual patterns of behavior
- unearth your authentic self and its values
- rewire outdated internal 'circuitry'
- summon the will to take action on your own behalf
- value and create opportunities for new experiences.

Devote a notebook or journal to this reboot project and answer all the questions in it. Writing is a much underrated growth strategy. Writing will better help you identify where and how you reached an impasse and how you can now move forward. We will talk more about the importance of documenting your reboot process and interesting ways to do so in Chapter 3.

If you balk at the idea of answering questions by writing in a journal, it does not mean that you cannot extract benefit from considering each of them. Our minds are like a search-engine. Contemplate a question and your mind will automatically search for answers. This process of answering introspective questions will disrupt and invalidate outdated internal files and update your current operating program – to help effect a relaunch into life.

Questions > Searches > Answers > More Questions > Reflection> Receptivity > Insight > Motivation > Intent > Action > Reboot> New Life

This book is not only full of growth-prompting questions, but since I am an incorrigible quote collector, it is also full of inspiring quotations at the end of each chapter, starting here:

## Quotations to Inspire the Need for a Reboot

*"The marvelous thing about a good question is that it shapes our identity as much by the asking as it does by the answering."*
- David Whyte

*"A life can be shattered in a single moment. It's normal to want instant repair. But the piecing back together requires befriending every jagged edge and sharp corner. And the scars seen in the end will tell not of the shattering, but of the resilience and value of the life."* - Wade Mullen

*"A bridge can still be built, while the bitter waters are flowing beneath."*
- Anthony Liccione

*"When we tackle obstacles, we find hidden reserves of courage and resilience we did not know we had. And it is only when we are faced with failure do we realize that these resources were always there within us. We only need to find them and move on with our lives."*
- A.P.J. Abdul Kalam

# 2. REVIEW

Review definition: "...*to look back on; to examine or study again; to take a retrospective of; a critical evaluation.*" Merriam-Webster

I N ORDER TO move forward, you first have to stop and take a serious look at where you have been – at what went before – at how you ended up where you are now. A review of your personal history and relationship with a high-control person or group is a way to begin to detect the sources of any paralysis problems and possible solutions – similar to a virus scanner on a computer that traces what is corrupting the files and impeding full functioning. This chapter will help you scan, review, rethink, and re-evaluate your experience both in and once out of the traumatic situation.

As you review your past, your walking away, and your recovery process, you will discover what might not have been addressed or what old files are still running without your direct awareness. You will also see just how far you have come, discover unacknowledged strengths, and pull the curtain back on long repressed needs, desires and longings.

During this review you may become aware that the story you have been telling yourself about your life is one mainly of grievance – understandably so. However, if you constantly ruminate on all the grievances of a lifetime you are, without realizing it, reinforcing a life-script of trauma, dysfunction, and disappointment. Since what you focus your attention upon tends to grow, you need to rethink any current settings of rumination on regrets and grievances.

However, to disrupt the old story of regrets and resentments it first needs to be told in its entirety. You have to call up all the hidden files. You have to fully and truthfully tell the story in order to adjust or update its settings. Only once you have told it (grievances and all) are you liberated to construct a new narrative that serves you, instead of being unconsciously controlled by one that wears you down and keeps you stuck.

Reviewing your story in this way may reveal that you are now in a new healing crisis, experiencing post-trauma paralysis or recovery fatigue. Neither situation is a statement of your self-worth. It is typical of any recovery process to take two steps forward and one step back. Pain and grief are most often resolved in a non-linear, spiral-like process.

Often, even after having reclaimed your authentic self, buried pain/grief may re-emerge due to being triggered by unforeseen circumstances. As best you can, go with the flow and avoid interpreting new pain or feelings of being stuck as any negative reflection on yourself.

You need to revisit the historical details of your entire traumatic experience to see what insights emerge for you. Perhaps you thought you would automatically revitalize your life when you left the intolerable situation, but with time and distance you see you need more advanced strategies to help acknowledge unresolved feelings, toss the regrets and resentments, release the pain, establish new patterns, refresh settings, build plans, and move on.

Ask yourself, what *is* the story that I tell about my life? Whether you realize it or not, you are living your life in accord with the narrative you tell yourself and others, and in accord with any hidden nuances that may only come to light with such a serious review and recounting.

Conducting this review will help determine whether the story you tell about your life has caught up with the actuality of your life now. If it has not, you will probably be experiencing inner conflict and old pain that is bound to haunt you and make you feel stuck. The inertia you are experiencing could simply be that you are still stuck in the old story. This reboot will help you come up-to-date with who you are now and the possibilities that are open to you.

Joan Borysenko, Ph.D. tells us that examining and rewriting our stories is *"narrative medicine"*. She says that when we see the negative effects of our old story and realize how tired we are of the way it constricts our life, we then have the motivation and power to create a new narrative. When we change our story, our patterns and behaviors change with it. Reviewing the story we tell ourselves about our life is powerful reboot medicine!

As a therapist I often find that one of my main tasks is to reflect back to the client, who they actually are now. Many who feel troubled and burdened are dragging around an old, outdated view of themselves based on an old, weary story of their life that is neither completely current nor accurate. Many of us are walking around in shoes too small. When you tell or write down your old, unexamined story, its inaccuracies and limitations become visible.

Charles Eisenstein, author of the book *The More Beautiful World Our Hearts Know is Possible*, says that to render an old story *"inoperative"*, you have to *"disrupt"* it. To disrupt an old story, he says, you first have to make it *"visible"*. How do you make it visible? By reviewing it. By making it explicit. By truthfully recording it.

Review and write about your personal history of abuse – your history of being exploited and/or abused, getting away, and experiences once free from the coercive situation. View it as taking healing, even if unpalatable, medicine.

If you haven't already, consider using a specially-designated journal to write your story – whether a story of being in an abusive family, controlling relationship, or coercive group. Here are just a few of the possible benefits of documenting your history in a journal:

- It will be a therapeutic, reparative exercise.
- It will help you take a step back from the story rather than being swallowed up by it.
- With the distance and perspective of writing, more insights and options will open up to you.

- As you write, you may see tangible evidence of how you may have been:
  - limiting yourself
  - inflexible or rigid
  - unconsciously participating in keeping yourself stuck
  - avoiding movement forward – without even realizing it.
- You may discover inaccurate interpretations you ascribe to your stuck state.
- You will see more clearly feelings that are evoked by perceiving that you are stuck.
- New understanding and compassion for your paralysis and/or fatigue will be evoked.
- You should discover some of the next steps in your post-trauma journey.

The next chapter of this book will give you many specific suggestions on *how* you can document or record the story of your 'captivity', 'escape', trauma, recovery, and efforts to move on. Writing is a powerful, well-researched technique to help you move past the stuckness of survival mode and to pull all the threads of your story into a more comprehensive whole – finally making sense of all the experiences that have brought you to this moment.

While this book cannot work through *all* your unaddressed 'corrupted files', it can help you get them out on the table where you can see them, assess them, decide what to do about them, and determine not to let them impede your movement forward.

By the way, it is possible to review your old story while creating a new, full life for yourself. Thousands are doing both right now.

## HOW I BENEFITED FROM WRITING MY STORY

After I faded from the Jehovah's Witness organization, struggled for several years on my own, worked up the courage to enter university, and gifted myself with personal therapy, I thought I was getting on with my life and rarely gave the oppressive cult and my years in it much thought. The only conscious thinking or feelings about anything to do with the cult were related to the pain of being shunned by my family of origin.

After raising children, and working as a psychotherapist for over twenty years, my husband and I found a piece of woodland property with a babbling brook carving around its border and a lovely, little house nestled in its hills. It was beyond perfect … for us. Family and friends lived in the region. We each had a home office for work we loved. We were free of cult controls. Life was good.

Soon after moving, I decided to read an exposé book by a former head of the Jehovah's Witnesses organization, Raymond Franz. Reading his book, *"Crisis of Conscience"* was a cathartic experience. It evoked reactions I did not expect. As I read, tears often streamed down my face. So much of what I had intuited and struggled with on my own while in the cult and while trying to leave it was validated on those pages … all these years later.

The feelings that came up, all these years later, in spite of having created a good free life, were evidence my recovery was not quite as complete as I had thought. I still had issues about having had so much of my life stolen and exploited. I was still harboring regrets and resentments. There was more work to do. I did it.

A few years later, after discovering a few ex-JW videos on YouTube I realized there were thousands now leaving the JW organization and struggling to recover from its abuses. Knowing I had the education, professional credentials and experience to help people recover from trauma, loss, and grief, as well as the same abusive, high-control past experience, I decided to write a book to help ex-JWs with their recovery. That book, *"Exiting the JW Cult: A Healing Handbook"* has proved to be a help to many. A year later I wrote my recollections of being a Jehovah's Witness and of prying my way free, entitled *"Fading Out of the JW Cult: A Memoir"*.

The actual writing of those two books provided an unexpected side benefit – the opportunity to revisit, review, take an inventory of, and re-evaluate my life in the cult, the struggle to exit, and the work to heal. The act of writing confirmed that my recovery was still not quite as complete as I believed. Rarely do healing and recovery proceed in a linear line – "*start here*" and "*end there*". Healing is not just a thing we can will or command. In fact, healing occurs like a spiral where we circle back later to re-address the same issues with a higher level of awareness.

All my work as a psychotherapist also taught me that the psyche of each person monitors their healing journey – judging how much 'excavation' and grieving a person can tolerate at a given time – and when we might be ready for more. It seemed I was ready for more.

It is not unusual to have people come back to therapy for a "reboot" as issues they thought they had addressed re-emerge (spiral around) asking for healing at a deeper level. Reboots or "*tune-ups*" are something we all need to do – probably more than once. As I reviewed my trauma history when writing those two books, I discovered that I was no exception to that rule.

Reflecting on my story, it suddenly became clear how much I had minimized the effects of all the restrictions and controls Jehovah's Witnesses impose on their members. *Minimization*, I discovered, was one of my most-used, unconscious coping mechanisms.

Believing I had worked through most of the losses and attending grief, I assumed that building a good simple life, along with the personal work in therapy, was all the reparative work I needed. It was the specific act of reviewing my story by writing it down that pried open a few of the doors I had prematurely closed – releasing still unresolved contents I had minimized (denied) and set outside of conscious awareness. What a gift that writing was!

One other benefit from reviewing and writing my story was that I saw that some trauma and pain that I attributed to being raised in a cult was actually due to being abandoned by my father during the same time period. I had conflated the two traumatic experiences. It was helpful to spend time teasing apart what pain belonged where. Once I did that, I discovered that I had also minimized the impact of the abandonment by my father and never knowing what had become of him. I was spiraling around passing through old, familiar territory learning there was more healing work to do with my growing level of awareness and ego strength.

I also realized that while a member of the cult, I had developed this defense of denial or minimization, when it came to my wants and needs. We were carefully taught that wishes, needs, wants, questions, ideas, were of little importance and should be set aside to accommodate the greater imperatives of the organization and Almighty God. Accordingly, if any personal concerns or longings reared their ugly head I quickly categorized them as insignificant compared to the "*kingdom work*" to which I had been told we were "*called*".

## HOW THE EGO DEFENDS US AGAINST WHAT SEEMS TOO HARD TO BEAR

Minimizing (a form of denial) became easy – so easy I was unaware that I was doing it. It became an automatic, unconscious, defensive reflex. The ego defense processes of minimizing and suppressing became second nature to me – and I had no conscious awareness of using these protective maneuvers. I minimized needs/desires and suppressed/repressed pain.

All the reactions, needs, desires and feelings that I suppressed however, waited inside eventually demanding attention. By writing two books, my psyche was signaled that I was stronger and ready to do a deeper level of healing work. *Writing* was the key to opening myself up to a higher level of awareness, a deeper level of healing, and a new level of operation.

All therapists know that ego defenses (such as denial, suppression, repression, avoidance, projection, intellectualization, rationalization) are initiated by the unconscious and that they serve a useful purpose – for a time. They protect the ego from being overwhelmed by events, inner conflicts, pain, problems, and the feelings that surround them.

A certain amount of denial and repression allow us to function while coping with loss and suffering. These coping mechanisms are called "ego defenses" because they defend the ego from the debilitating anxiety that emerges when it becomes aware of fears, feelings, pain, frailties, existential dread, or personal character flaws.

What every therapist and client need to tease apart is just how much habitual ego defenses are interfering with resolving inner conflicts and interfering with living a full life. Ego defenses may help and protect us in the moment, but if we don't come to terms with the difficult experience it may come back to haunt us – as in the case when suddenly we feel overwhelmed, anxious, angry, stuck or unable to move forward with life. The ego defenses themselves can become problems in their own right.

Before going any further, allow me to describe exactly what the ego is: It is not an actual part of the body/mind but is a term used to describe a certain *function* of the body/mind. It is the part of the personality that is experienced as "oneself". We need a strong, healthy ego function to cope with life's challenges.

This ego function helps us think critically and test reality. It also performs certain defensive measures that help us cope when reality threatens to overwhelm. *Ego defenses* are meant to be a temporary assistance or protection. For example, if we are in denial about how abusive our partner is – the denial may drop away as reality cannot be ignored and as the ego feels more able to take a stand for itself.

The optimal state is to be able to act with a strong, autonomous ego. Having ego strength is desirable and has nothing to do with narcissism. Narcissism is an inflated ego function defending itself against wounded attachment issues, a sense of emptiness, self-doubt, low self-esteem, and even self-loathing. A 'strong' ego is a healthy, resilient one – one in touch with reality and equipped to cope with it. Resilience is another term for ego strength. We will return to discussing the ego and its resilience a bit more in Chapters 4 and 10.

## THE STORY I NEEDED TO REVIEW AND RETHINK

I had done effective work in personal therapy, but a couple of my therapists seemed to almost validate my habit of minimizing needs and pain. (I saw several therapists, some because of my personal desire to heal and others as a requirement of courses in psychology at university and other schools of therapy such as Gestalt and Psychosynthesis.) Things they said implied that *"the experience was now in the past* (life in the cult and adapting once out) *and that I seemed to be thriving and surely it was time to just get over it and move on."* That's exactly what I wanted to do. I wanted to just get over it. I wanted to minimize it and move on with my life as a wife, mother, student, professional – which did not leave time for dredging up old hurts or losses. I kept a lid on a well of repressed pain and rage – with good, old denial.

The story I told myself at that point was that I had bounced back, my grieving was done, and my life was now devoted to gaining all the learning and experience I needed to become a psychotherapist. It was a story that made me feel good and comforted me, for at many points I had believed I would never be able to make up for the way the J.W. organization keeps its members from meeting their potential.

I was unaware at that point that my ego defense of minimization (denial) had stalled my chances at a complete recovery and had possibly put a cap on just how far I could move forward. Certain corrupt files had been buried and unbeknownst to me I was still dragging them around. No wonder I felt so fatigued! Again, I discovered these things due to the simple act of writing.

As said, Charles Eisenstein suggests we have to *"disrupt"* our old story to fully step into a new one and I discovered the act of writing down my old story, all those years later, was an important act of disruption.

My well-honed old narrative, replete with unconscious minimization, was disrupted by realizing that things that happened to me in the coercive group were more significant than I had believed and that certain of my mild reactions did not match the gravity of the events or situations. The act of writing down my story became an opportunity for awakening to the fact that I harbored corrupt files in old psychological settings.

Our stories become the lens thru which we see and intersect with the world. Our life is filtered through the lens of the story we continue to tell our self about what things mean or meant, and what is still possible for us.

Perhaps it is time to review and reconsider the story you tell your-self about your life, your wounds, your disappointments, your regrets, your resentments, any paralysis, and your efforts to move forward with your life.

When you feel stuck, it may be that you are unconsciously living by the assumptions, rules and roles of an old story - one that was, perhaps, never really yours. Get your story down on paper and see! This book and its questions are designed to help you disrupt the old narrative or script and create a new, true one – replacing corrupted files with new, updated ones.

You will also derive benefit by writing down your answers to many of the questions provided in this book. But first, pull out your note-book or journal and write down a reader's digest version of for exam-ple, your time in a cult, wanting to leave, leaving, and the aftermath of leaving.

Then, after your unique story is in a basic written form you can review, assess, reflect upon, and write about your feelings, beliefs, blocks, fears, etc. using the questions in this book. This can be a sweet, private, powerful way of initiating a reboot.

There are 350+ questions scattered throughout the twelve chap-ters of this reboot book. (The numbering of the questions continues in sequence throughout all the chapters rather than starting anew with #1 in each chapter. This will help you better note and cross-reference them in your journal.)

Poet David Whyte in his collection of poetry entitled, *Everything Is Waiting for You,* speaks of the importance of questions in his poem *"Sometimes"*, which I share parts of here:

*Sometimes ...*
*you come to a place whose only task is to trouble you*
*with tiny but frightening requests ...*
*Requests to stop what you are doing right now*
*and ...*
*questions that can make ... a life ...*

Of course, you cannot work through all of the questions provided here at once. Give the book and the questions a read through and then using your reboot journal go back and work with the questions. Some of the questions may not apply to you or your circumstances. There will be many more that do. (*Therapist's tip:* Questions you automatically dismiss or resist are often the very ones that you most need to address.)

Each question is about you and your experience. Each question will be answered privately, in service of personal renewal. The questions are not a test. The only way you can do this wrong is if you don't do it!

Time to begin.

## QUESTIONS ABOUT BEING STUCK:

1. Describe exactly how you feel stuck, stalled or at an impasse.

2. Have you had previous experiences of feeling stuck? Describe them.

3. Do you criticize or negate yourself for being stuck? How exactly?

4. Can you name the ways being stuck may have helped/help you?

5. How did you move past previous feelings of stuckness?

6. Can you use what you did then, now? How?

7. Are there ways that it serves you to be stuck?

8. What do you imagine might happen if you were no longer stuck?

9. Does what you imagine in question #8 scare you or excite you? Describe.

10. If being stuck scares you, does the fear originate with your inner child or with the adult you?

11. Is there a part of you that does not believe you are deserving of moving forward in life?

12. When and how exactly did this impasse toward a full, free life occur?

13.   What was happening in your life at that time? How might it/they be related?

14.   Do the above questions provide clues to what needs to be addressed to get unstuck?

15.   How can you better address these issues now?

16.   What internal images accompany this feeling of stuckness (look to dreams, books, songs movies, etc.)? Timothy Butler tells us, *"The image is a messenger for a larger paradigm than the one you have in mind."* Transpersonal psychologist James Hillman encourages his clients to *"follow the image"*, inferring the image often holds the key to the next step.

17.   How do these internal images make you feel? Can you illustrate them in your journal?

18.   What do you learn about yourself and your recovery process from those images?

19.   Can you begin to observe and name the patterns, habits, thoughts, or behaviors that keep you stuck? (Keep a dated record of them in your journal. It may be helpful to look back at what you've written if you encounter any future fatigue or paralysis.)

20.   What is the message contained in your feeling of "stuckness" or impasse?

21.   How may this stuck feeling be an important passage for you?

22.   What have you learned from being stuck that you could carry forward to benefit the rest of your life?

23.   Is there a part of you that perceives you are taking care of yourself (e.g. securing your safety) by being stuck? Explore.

24.   Have you really grasped there is nothing 'wrong' with you because you are stuck?

25.   Can you demonstrate understanding and compassion toward the part of you that is stuck, just as you would toward someone else who feels stuck? Consider writing a letter to the part of you that feels stuck.

## QUESTIONS TO HELP YOU BEGIN TO RE-EXAMINE YOUR WRITTEN STORY:

26. Can you open up space in your mind to be curious about the habitual story you tell yourself regarding your traumatic past, escaping from it, and what that means for you now? In order to answer the rest of the questions in this book, get out your journal and first write the story of your trauma-ridden history if you have not done so already.

27. In just a few phrases, summarize the story you tell yourself about your life, especially as it relates to high levels of control, exploitation, trauma, or abuse.

28. If you were to give your story a title, what would it be?

29. Can you divide the story into stages, phases, episodes or chapters? Write them down.

30. Is the current part of the story of your life still preoccupied with the abuse or the coercive group?

31. In your story, what seem to be the most significant complaints or grievances?

32. In your story, what are the most significant regrets?

33. In your narrative, what seem to be the most significant wounds?

34. What events or feelings might you be minimizing, ignoring, or setting aside as unimportant?

35. What elements about your traumatic experience still remain unsaid or unexpressed?

36. How does it feel to examine and confront any untold experiences?

37. Is your story full of fears, regrets, unmet needs, longings and resentments? Describe.

38. Does the answer for question #37 manifest in or affect your life now? How?

39. Have you created a safe inner space (body/mind) and a safe

outer space (immediate environment) where you can work on creating a new narrative – and work on this reboot?

## QUESTIONS TO HELP UNDERSTAND HOW YOU ARE AFFECTED BY A TRAUMATIC PAST:

40.  In your narrative do you label yourself a victim or a survivor?

41.  How are you attached to a story of being a victim ... and could that be holding you back?

42.  What would it take for you to be able to let go of the descriptors "victim" or "survivor"?

43.  Are you willing to examine and question any default assumptions, perceptions, impulses, habits, thinking patterns that may be at the root of your impasse? For example:

- Do you continue a cult or family exigency to isolate yourself from the world?

- Do you find it difficult to trust?

- Do you continue to judge people and situations based on the views of your family or the coercive group?

- Do you harbor doubts and/or guilt about your choice to leave?

- Do you find it difficult to act on your own behalf and find yourself wanting someone else to map the way, do it for you, or constantly reassure you?

- Because of the stance of helplessness learned in coercive systems do you now suffer from low self-esteem?

44.  Do you realize you are stronger now and can look more closely at your wounds? Give a few examples of how you are stronger now.

45.  Do you realize that speaking the truth about the lies, controls, and indignities is essential for healing and independence?

46. How might you have minimized the amount of healing work you have done or still need to do to recover and move ahead?

47. Are you, perhaps, keeping secrets to protect yourself or someone else?

48. For example, how might you have repressed or glossed over incidents of sexism, sexual abuse, racism, misogyny, homophobia, and/or physical abuse?

49. How might any such events (question #48) be affecting your ability to let go, move on, and create your own independent life?

50. Has it occurred to you that suppressing what you experienced and how you *really* felt/feel is something you were groomed to do by the organization or a family system ... and no longer need to do?

51. How would addressing these difficult issues – now – help you move on from this impasse?

52. Are mysterious physical ailments trying to tell you to look deeper ... what might such ailments symbolize or be 'saying' to you? Look for the metaphors.

53. How have you worked through any guilt, anger, and remaining grief?

54. How have you learned to manage any lingering distress, doubt, fears, or pain?

55. Where might you be attached to old patterns and ways of being, learned in the past?

56. What do you fear most about this reboot process?

57. Is that fear left over from the past? Do you want to be governed by trauma-related fears?

58. In what ways might you still be attached to old beliefs, habits, patterns, fears?

59. In what ways are you attached to patterns you established for

your life after claiming your freedom? For example, might you be attached to a pattern of avoidance?

60. Have patterns that at one point offered you stability in the midst of chaos now become rigid and an obstacle to moving forward?

61. In other words, can you examine the patterns put in place to facilitate your recovery that may now be a barrier and keeping you stuck?

62. What lingering vulnerabilities or sensitivities might be keeping you stuck?

63. How old do you feel inside when you experience vulnerability or sensitivity? (It is hard to do the work of recovery or a reboot when feeling 'little' inside. Therapy could be of help here.)

64. Can you be understanding and kind to the part of you that feels vulnerable and is, perhaps, afraid of moving forward? Describe how.

65. What rationalizations or defenses (avoidance, denial, rage, control, rigidity, etc.) are you using to avoid completing the grieving, letting go, or moving on process?

66. What fears or unacknowledged needs might lie underneath any rationalizations?

67. Could what you are interpreting as "fear" actually be the anxiety of sensing an 'emergency' state of fight or flight or freeze?

68. Are you aware that people stuck in the "freeze" state often describe it as a sense of collapse or helplessness?

69. Can you challenge the truth of the perception that you are helpless?

70. Are there opportunities that are seemingly invisible to you, due perhaps to your fears?

71. Are you, perhaps, afraid of the very thing you long for – freedom?

72. Are you aware unconscious fears can create inner conflicts that paralyze you?

73. Is it possible you are not only still viewing the world through the lens of family or cult indoctrination but are also inadvertently recreating that 'world' in the present?

74. How does any anger about your losses trap you into being over-ly-sensitive or reactive?

75. Are you unwittingly in a war against yourself? How are you con-flicted - within?

76. Do you find you have a pattern of avoiding anything that seems risky or difficult?

77. Are you able to set limits and say "No"? Are you able to say "Yes" to opportunities?

78. How might you have allowed yourself to remain consumed with rage?

79. Are you a grievance collector?

80. Are you expecting a new life and new opportunities while still operating from old indoctrination and ways of being?

81. Do you see how unconscious attachment to old beliefs or behaviors diminishes you, your sense of self, and your sense of agency in the world?

82. How are you looking for substitute supports like those you had in the controlling system?

83. How might unresolved grief be rearing its head asking for atten-tion and making you think you are stuck when, in fact, you just have more grieving to do?

84. Have you recognized any inadequacies of your current mental model of the world and how you believe things should operate?

85. How do you need to change your current mental model of how the world operates and what you are capable of in it?

## QUESTIONS TO HELP YOU REFLECT UPON
## WHAT *IS* WORKING FOR YOU NOW:

86. What recovery work have you actually done for yourself since leaving?

87. What feels complete in terms of your recovery?

88. What still does not feel resolved for you?

89. What IS working well for you in your life now?

90. What is not working for you?

91. What small steps can you take now with regard to what is not working — things you have just not tackled yet?

92. What are you especially grateful for now?

93. Have you caught up with who you really are now — beyond an abuse survivor or beyond a cult devotee/victim/survivor?

94. What new qualities, skills, and competencies have you developed since leaving the group?

95. What new qualities, skills, and competencies would you like to develop?

96. Do you have realistic expectations about what recovery and freedom look like?

97. Describe what you expect. Evaluate these expectations. Are they reasonable?

98. How can you take up this final push to recover and move on?

99. Is there a part of you that is too proud or too vulnerable to allow anyone else to provide the help you need to get unstuck?

100. Can you turn trauma into triumph by owning and exercising your right to decide and act on your own behalf?

101. What unconscious or unreasonable limitations might you have placed upon yourself?

102. What unreasonable demands or expectations have you placed upon yourself?

103. Have you been looking for support in places or with people that actually hold you back?

104. Could you be in need of the support, positive mirroring, and an unconditional holding environment that therapy would provide?

105. Can you lovingly open the door to all you have repressed and avoided without condemning yourself in the process? Do you need a therapist to help you do this?

106. What were you doing at times when you felt the most like your best, authentic self?

107. If you were to imagine people celebrating you and saying wonderful things about you, what positive things do you imagine they would be saying? Take a moment to soak that in.

108. Are there clues in your answers to the last two questions about what really matters to you? Write down and reflect upon what comes to mind.

109. Are there any changes you could make to operationalize these things that matter to you?

110. What is the greatest gift you could give yourself right now? Are you willing to give it?

Linda Graham, in her book *"Bouncing Back"* encourages us to write about our trauma:

*"Acceptance involves no blame or shame: it allows us to honor and accept an entire event and integrate it into our sense of self. We can do so by creating a narrative of the event with the following components:*

- *This is what happened.*
- *This is what I did to survive it (understandable, even brilliant)*
- *This has been the cost (compassion makes it safe enough to even look at that).*
- *This is what I have learned (a new narrative of self that allow us to live with, even be proud of ourselves).*

- *This is how I respond to life now (be resilient going forward)."*
  (bullet points added)

Record the above five bulleted statements of Linda Graham in your *Reboot Journal,* write about them and go back and refer to them often. They will help orient you as you write your story, as you review and accept what happened, assess the cost, understand the measures you took to survive, acknowledge all you have learned, and develop new ways of responding to life now.

You will certainly have some regrets about the time lost and opportunities missed while being in a controlling family dynamic or coercive group. What you want to avoid is having regrets about what you are doing or not doing *now*!

In a 2015 interview with the website *Salon*, existential psychiatrist Irvin D. Yalom, M.D., referencing his book *"Creatures of a Day"*, speaks about the importance of living a life without regrets about actions in the past. Undoubtedly, we may have regrets about the years we gave up to a cult or an abusive relationship, but Yalom rightly asks:

- *"What's your life right now?*

- *If we were to meet a year or two from now what new regrets would you have built up?*

- *How could you go about constructing a regret-free life for your-self?"*  (bullet points added)

Reviewing and recording the story about your experience with trauma or abuse and answering the above questions to help you think more deeply about how you were affected, then and now, is the first step in moving past feeling stuck. Reviewing and recording your story will also help you *"construct a regret-free life for yourself"*. Take your time with this review, it may contain the clues, answers, pointers, *"aha"* insights, release, and even internal permission you need to move forward with your life.

## Quotations to Inspire You About the Need to Review Your Story:

*"I looked hard at my faith, my friendships, my work, my sexuality, my entire life and asked:*

- *How much of this was my idea?*
- *Do I truly want any of this, or is this what I was conditioned to want?*
- *Which of my beliefs are of my own creation and which were programmed into me?*
- *How much of who I've become is inherent, and how much was just inherited? ...*
- *Who was I before I became who the world told me to be?*

*Over time, I walked away from my cages. I slowly built a new marriage, a new faith, a new worldview, a new purpose, a new family, and a new identity by design instead of default. From my imagination instead of my indoctrination."* - Glennon Doyle, *"Untamed"* (bullet points added)

*"A life impasse fulfills a specific purpose in our psychological development. It is a call to return to and integrate aspects of our emotional and psychological being that have been set aside because of competing life circumstances ..."* - Timothy Butler

*"... mine the wreckage for underlying strengths and key lessons."* - Jenny Blake

*"Fear is a question. What are you afraid of and why? Our fears are a treasure house of self-knowledge if we explore them."* - Marilyn French

**NOTE:** If thoughts of suicide due to being controlled, exploited, abused, deceived, rejected, shunned, stuck, and more, arise – please seek immediate help from a mental-health professional or call your local suicide lifeline or crisis intervention service.

USA call toll-free **1-800-273-TALK (8255)** for free service available 24/7 to anyone in suicidal crisis.

Crisis **Text Line**, USA: (all ages, 24/7) text: **HELLO to 741741**

CANADA call toll-free **1-833-456-4566**

Suicide crisis lifelines in other countries can be found here:
**http://www.suicide.org/international-suicide-hotlines.html**

# 3. RECORD

Record definition: "*...set down in writing ...*" Merriam-Webster

S OCIAL PSYCHOLOGIST JAMES W. Pennebaker and Dr. John Evans, in their book *"Expressive Writing: Words That Heal"*, say, *"... it may be beneficial to simply write about the event itself, how you felt when it was occurring, and how you feel now. As you write about this upheaval, you might begin to tie it to other parts of your life. For example,*

- *How is it related to your childhood and your relationships with your parents and close family?*

- *How is the event connected to those people you have most loved, feared, or been angry with?*

- *How is this upheaval related to your current life...?*

*And above all, how is this event related to who you have been in the past, who you would like to be in the future, and who you are now? ... "* (bullet points added)

In the last chapter I shared how I benefited from writing my story, wanting to encourage you to review and reassess yours by doing the same. Start to journal about your traumatic life experience now, if you have not yet. Just thinking about it is not enough. You will not tap the depth of personal significance and accompanying feelings by simply thinking about it.

Write down the narrative of your past, how it affected you, your struggle to leave it all behind, the after-effects of leaving, your work to recover, and any ways you feel your history is still affecting you now. You don't have to go into every minute detail, just get down the basic facts, even in point form. You can always go back and fill in any details you deem important later.

Don't be intimidated by this task. Simply document the most important recollections – one at a time – like the headings of a book. Leave spaces after each heading and come back later to fill in the details. Experiences do not have to be recorded in the order in which they occurred. You can organize them later. Simply get significant events down on paper as they come to mind (recording the date or time period when they happened). Do it in bullet form if you choose. You do not have to do it all in one sitting. Do it your way, in any sequence, according to your own timetable and style.

Writing down your story and documenting your wounds, your accomplishments, your disappointments, your reactions, your hopes, and your intentions, etc. is not only revelatory, but profoundly healing. Julia Cameron, author of "*The Artist's Way*" says:

> "*Writing is medicine. It is an appropriate antidote to injury.*
> *It is an appropriate companion for any difficult change.*"

Do set aside any resistance you may have to keeping a written journal during your reboot journey. There is actually a form of therapy called "*Narrative Therapy*", based on the multiple benefits of having people tell and/or write the story of their life. The act of putting your story in writing helps you externalize it, acknowledge the aftereffects, and see it with more objectivity – with a fresh perspective.

Another goal of narrative therapy is to interrupt or disrupt the old dominant story and its deep-rutted neural pathways in your brain. As you write, you may realize you are now writing as someone who courageously freed themselves from coercive control. Owning that realization, will help rewire your brain to feel empowered and ready to take on new challenges.

While it is not *absolutely* essential to write to reboot, writing will help you push ahead with, and solidly anchor, this reboot project. You will reap so many benefits that you may continue to journal even after the reboot! Everyone's story deserves to be told. Poet, Maya Angelou said:

*"There is no greater agony than bearing an untold story inside you."*

Externalize your story by putting it down on paper and enjoy the relief that externalization brings you. Don't wait. Life is inviting you to do it now. When we don't have a therapist or a trusted confidante, we always have paper and pen. Professor of Education, Brad Wilcox says, *"A personal journal is an ideal environment in which to become. It is a perfect place for you to think, feel, discover, expand, remember, and dream."*

Novelist and poet, Jim Harrison compares his journal to a gold mine: *"Your subconscious mind is trying to help you all the time. That's why I keep a journal – not for chatter but mostly for the images that flow into the mind or little ideas … so it's like your gold mine when you start writing."*

Social psychologist, James Pennebaker, Ph.D. and Joshua M. Smyth, Ph.D. in their book *"Opening Up by Writing It Down: How Expressive Writing Improves Health and Eases Emotional Pain"*, recount a simple research experiment where traumatized people were asked to do automatic, free-form writing for 15 minutes a day, for 3 to 4 days in a row. They were instructed to write without censoring, judging, correcting, or worrying about having anyone else see it. Those who participated in this experiment felt significantly less traumatized after the assignment and had more insight about the events of the story and their feelings about it. Their journal writing also helped alleviate some depressive symptoms and some mild physical ailments. Journaling can be a profound act of self-care. Pennebaker also refers to journaling or expressive writing as a form of *"course correction"*, which sounds like a reboot to me.

After any experience in which we are controlled, not allowed to be ourselves, deceived, exploited, or abused, we need to tell the story. Telling it is a form of psychological debriefing. The telling does not have to be public. Your body/mind will be satisfied with the private act of writing it down.

Julie Gray, founder of Stories Without Borders tells us, "*People who have experienced trauma in their lives, whether or not they consider themselves writers, can benefit from creating narratives out of their stories. It is helpful to write it down ... in safety and non-judgment. Trauma can be quite isolating. Those who have suffered need to understand how they feel.*" One of the best ways to deepen your understanding of your own story is to take the time to write it down.

Find a notebook or journal and consider labeling it something like: "*My Reboot Journal*" - "*My Moving Forward Journal*" - "*Documenting My Progress*" - "*Course Correction*". It will be a reboot companion that helps you review, re-examine, reconsider, and disrupt any paralyzing effects of your painful history. You will surely discover pieces of your current puzzle of stuckness that reveal the bigger picture and point to the path ahead. (There is a companion journal to this book, entitled, "*My Reboot Journal*" that provides prompts, images, quotations and all 350+ questions from this book in the back of the journal. This journal/workbook is designed to facilitate or ease the writing of your story and the documenting of your reboot process with a format designed for the purpose.)

Some may mistakenly think a reboot journal has to be like a diary requiring them to give an account of every day. A reboot journal is not like that. You do not have to write in it giving a quotidian account of every banal activity. It is not a daily diary. Use it when you have something significant to write about your past, your feelings, insights you want to add, and when answering the questions or doing the exercises in this book.

A reboot journal will, in effect, be the beginning of the final leg of your journey to a full, free life. As said, there are many therapists, such as Carl Jung, Ira Progoff, James Pennebaker, Christina Baldwin, Elizabeth Warson, Joan Borysenko, Susan Borkin, Lucia Capacchione, and Cathy Malchiodi, who have researched and recommend the tried and true technique of journaling to help manage emotions and any stress after trauma. Those therapists strongly recommend writing a complete narrative of the trauma endured (emotional, psychological, spiritual, physical, and/or sexual) including how you coped and what you learned.

If you can, end your narrative of the control, exploitation and loss with the ways you have benefited by leaving the controlling situation. Psychologist, Rick Hanson tells us we can change the structure of our brain for the better (neuroplasticity) by *"marinating" in good experiences* which allow the brain's neurons to rewire. Hanson calls it *"hardwiring for happiness"*.

You can marinate in good experiences and reset your brain away from trauma and any resulting impasse in the same journal where you document the trauma and/or abuses.

A reboot journal is also a place where you can:

- record current issues you are dealing with and the feelings these issues produce
- record entries of only a word or two combined with an image – e.g. using point form when you don't feel like writing sentences or paragraphs
- write recovery-related stream of consciousness thoughts
- include descriptions of relevant dreams (even if you do not understand them yet)

- include images to illustrate what happened and how you really feel on the inside

- scan photos of yourself or significant people/places, and glue them beside the text

- use prompts such as *"Lists of 10 Things"*, for example:

  - 10 vague memories that seem significant

  - 10 events that still feel unresolved

  - 10 things accomplished since walking away from control

  - 10 things on my post-trauma, now-free bucket list

- use pages of your journal to 'confront' people who exploited or abused you, saying what you might otherwise never get the chance to express

- use pages to describe what now inspires and pleases you

- record affirmations or inspiring quotations that keep you in a positive mindset – words/phrases/poems that you can turn to in moments of discouragement

- write a compassionate letter to your child self or self trapped in the coercive group

- draw images with your non-dominant hand which can produce insights without the judgments and edits of the evaluating left-brain which is in charge when writing with your dominant hand

- answer all the questions and do other exercises suggested throughout this book – such as the exercise below.

In a reboot journal where you are working out why you feel stuck and what you need to do to move forward, one example of a visual exercise you can include is a *timeline of your life* – one where you make a line representing the trajectory your life from birth to death. Then you mark on that timeline the years when significant life events occurred. The most significant mark, however, is where you think you are *now* on that line between life and death.

This little, yet impactful exercise is quite sobering and can be used as motivation to release whatever is holding you back from full participation in life. It is a visual reminder of the amount of life you have left to heal, grow, reclaim your independence, and create the value, meaning, purpose and satisfaction you want for your life. Your birth to death timeline might look like this:

Sample Birth to Death Timeline

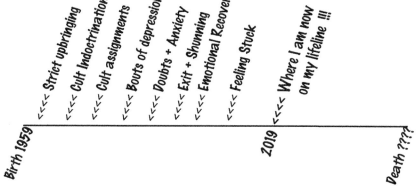

Timelines such as this are strong reminders of how fleeting life is ... how few years we really have left to create the connectedness, engagement, meaning and contentment we deserve. Timelines are an excellent incentive to release what we need to release and move on to make the most of the years left. Psychiatrist Irvin D. Yalom in his book, *"Becoming Myself: A Psychiatrist's Memoir"* says: *"This exercise rarely fails to incite deeper awareness of life's precious transiency."*

The perfect place for an exercise such as this is in your own journal – a writing journal, an art journal, an art therapy journal, a healing journal, a reboot journal – whatever form you choose. A blank template of this exercise is provided for you in the *"My Reboot Journal"* companion workbook.

## DESIGNING YOUR REBOOT JOURNAL

The ways to journal are as varied as the people who do. You will develop your preferred style of documenting your story and feelings. Whatever way you choose to explore the work you've done and have yet to do, it is a wonderful way to reboot and turn the page, so to speak. Allow me to share on these next few pages some exciting ways people are journaling these days. You may discover an option that appeals to you.

One advocate of journaling says: "*Journaling can also be a safe way to process traumatic elements of your abuse that you aren't yet ready to share with anyone else or even say out loud...Translating thoughts into words changes how our brains think about things...*"

Your journal will become a safe, even sacred, place; like a trusted confidante with whom you share your past, deepest concerns, secrets, and future aspirations. When each entry is dated it becomes a valuable record of your trauma experience, recovery, and reboot – evidence of how far you have come and how much further you have yet to go. Find alone time to make entries and keep the journal where no one can intrude on these private outpourings of your heart.

Some creative ways to journal are by creating or using:

- an art journal
- an art therapy journal
- a junk journal
- a bullet journal
- an altered book journal
- a journal consisting of letters you write to yourself, a friend, or to the journal itself
- a *"morning pages"* journal as created by Julia Cameron
- a dream journal
- a digital journal
- an online website or app designed for journaling
- a simple notebook or journal
- a sketch book
- or any combination of the above.

Let's explore some of these journaling options in a little more detail:

One intriguing way to journal is to use existing books and alter them using art materials such as paint and/or paper collage. In **altered book journaling**, you revamp an existing book by tearing out many of its original printed pages. (Search for YouTube videos that demonstrate how best to remove pages from a book which still conserves the strength of the book's spine.) Page removal makes space for the addition of collage materials or pockets where you can store important papers, notes, letters, memorabilia, etc. The addition of such papers and collage papers adds to the thickness of a page and therefore the book (hence the need to remove pages before you start). You write, collage, draw and/or paint on the pages remaining in the book, and end up creating an entirely new book by altering the existing one. There eventually remains very little of the original book.

Altered book journaling offers the mischievous option of using old books from the coercive group to work on your reboot. If the sweet irony of converting a book designed to control your life into a book you redesign to support your liberation appeals – an altered book journal is for you!

Imagine using a cult's publications and leaving portions of the text or images visible as a reminder of ludicrous theories, prophecies, and demands with which you felt you had to align yourself. Some of your journaling could be in direct response to the written words in the book that robbed you of time, energy and freedom. It could be enormously satisfying to alter the books that played a part in controlling your life, into journals of emancipation and transformation!

The process of turning an existing book into a visual journal provides a symbolic vehicle for exploring your life. It is a wonderful way to reflect upon your life, to disrupt the stuck patterns, to rewire your brain with a new experience, to express what you had to suppress, and to manage any difficult emotions as a result of trauma. Later, you can use the altered book to map out your future.

Art therapist Cathy Malchiodi, Ph.D. wrote an article in *Psychology Today* describing the process of altering an existing book into an art therapy book entitled, "*Altered Book and Visual Journaling: Changing the Story Through "Altered" Art Therapy and Visual Journaling*". In the article she defines altered books as: "... *a form of mixed media artwork that changes a book from its original form into something different, altering its appearance or intended meaning. The book itself can be cut, collaged, painted or otherwise changed or transformed in some way.*"

You do not have to be an artist to create any kind of art therapy journal or altered book journal. Some people paint in them with acrylic paint, gesso, watercolors, etc., some draw with pencils or markers, others draw using stick figures, and some doodle or color around their normal writing. Some take images from magazines and glue them in beside their own text. Some who decide to alter an old book use the text of the old book as the background and write and draw directly on top of that original text.

Every page of your journal does not have to have art, illustrations, collage or embellishments. You decide where and how to write about and/or illustrate your story of trauma, recovery, and reboot. It could be only every few pages that you add images, drawings or collage.

Of course, what is important is to get your story down in writing. The art and images are vehicles to enhance the therapeutic effects and to add interest, impact and dimension to your work. The artwork and craftwork of an altered book adds a new experience to your reboot process and, as you will learn, new experiences help rewire your brain away from old, limiting ones.

Coming out of a high-control situation, one of the things you probably had to repress or postpone was your innate creativity. I never knew I had a creative side until a friend urged me to try my hand at collage and painting. If I had not been willing to push past my initial resistance and make the attempt, there is much that would have remained unknown and unexplored. You, too, could discover an immensely satisfying form of creative expression by incorporating a bit of art, color, or paper collage into your journaling.

Cathy Malchiodi, also author of the *The Art Therapy Sourcebook*, tells us more about the value of visual journaling using altered books: "*From an art therapy perspective, creatively altering a book can be a form of rewriting one's life story through visual journaling. It is similar to the process of narrative therapy, but taking the approach a step further through redefining the story not only through words, but also images. Harriet Wadeson, a well-known art therapist, author and researcher, applied altered book journaling to her own struggles with cancer and describes the experience in her book, "Journaling Cancer in Words and Images" … Her altered book contains not only images of pain, suffering and the realities of illness and treatment, but also beauty, inspiration and transformation in words and symbols."*

Dr. Malchiodi herself followed Wadeson's example and used the process of altering a book into a visual journal to help with her recovery from a mild traumatic brain injury (TBI). She found it not only therapeutic but a comforting, relaxing diversion from the stress of recovery and reclaiming her life. As she worked on her journal, interspersing words and images, she enjoyed the benefits of relaxation provided by a sense of play and creativity while telling and illustrating the story of her travails and triumphs.

Malchiodi sums it up this way: *"All art making is in some way about transformation and renewal; altered art empowers the creator to restore what has been lost and make changes to what already exists through symbol and metaphor. In brief, my simple altered book not only helped to re-author the experience of mild TBI, it also empowered me to honor and transform my healing journey through art and image. "* An altered book cum journal will do that for you too.

Example of an altered book journal using photos, images and text.

Another popular form of journaling is "**junk journaling**". With a junk journal you use materials that would normally be consigned to the trash (old invoices, cereal boxes, tissue boxes, old letters, etc.) to create journal pages on which you can later add images that illustrate your text. There are instructional videos online to help you learn how to do all of this.

There are also **digital download journal kits** (decorated and lined pages to download and print) you can purchase on Etsy which you can use to create your own form of a journal. It's easier than you think! I've been making digital kit journals and altered book journals for a while now. If I can do it, so can you!

Of course, you do not have to use digital page designs or alter an existing book to create a visual journal. You can simply purchase **a blank journal** or **a lined notebook** that has pages sturdy enough to tolerate glue and cut images/papers pasted or collaged in the journal. (Peter Pauper Press makes journals with beautiful cover designs and strong interior pages.) There are notebooks with blank space at the top of the page and lines on the bottom half.

Another form of journaling is **the bullet journal** where you keep your entries brief using point form. You can still add illustrations, drawings and found images to a bullet journal.

You will decide how much imagery or collage you include in any journal. There is no right way or wrong way – just your way. A journal can be as edgy, raw, gorgeous or ungainly as you please. It is not done to be put on display or to show anyone else. It is just for you and is a very satisfying activity. It is also a way to add a bit of play and relaxation into the serious work of recording your story. To add images from magazines to illustrate your story, all you need are scissors and glue. Use markers or colored pens to write parts of your story around them.

**Digital journals** and **encrypted online journaling websites** are an option and there are now **journaling apps** for iPhone and iPad. However, when working digitally you lose the power and intimacy of the physical act of writing (using your hand holding a pen to make meaningful strokes has benefits). Still, digital journaling is a better option than not recording your story at all.

As previously mentioned, there is **a journal/workbook companion** to this reboot book entitled "My Reboot Journal – *A Reboot After Recovery from Trauma* Workbook Companion".

On my website https://www.bonniezieman.com there are several *Reboot Resources* including templates, posters, art-therapy journaling guidelines, art therapy journal and journal-making video links, and links to reboot-related, decorated and lined pages for making a coordinating journal, should you wish to make your own.

Journaling is a way to externalize fears, worries, and memories of trauma. It is a way to take the feelings out of your body/mind and store them on the page. The benefits of an expressive art journal are worth taking a step out of your usual comfort zone. Frequently we don't have any idea what we will enjoy or be good at until we give it a chance. Do give this a try!

Below is another of example of visual journaling – combining words and imagery that illustrate the person's feelings about the past, present, and hopes for the future.

"If your heart is broken, make art with the pieces."

- Shane Koyczan

If your immediate reaction to visual journaling is that you don't think turning your journal into a combo of text and imagery is your thing (although I encourage you to push past that initial resistance), you can still write out your story and use the questions in this book as prompts for exploring what is now keeping you from fully embracing your new life.

Russian philosopher George Gurdeiff says: *"Human beings live in a prison cell of their own creation. And almost everybody is content to re-arrange the furniture in their prison cell and to call it freedom."* You are not wasting time simply re-arranging the facts of your particular trauma by recording them in a journal. You are writing it all down to externalize it, to rewire your brain away from the trauma, to extract the learnings, to map out your new life, to leave the pain and paralysis on the page, to eventually close the book and walk away rebooted, relieved, empowered, and free.

## Quotations to Inspire you to Record the Story of Your Life:

*"What a comfort is this journal. I tell myself to myself and throw the burden on my book and feel relieved."* - Anne Lister

*"... memory is always a collaboration in progress."* - Richard Powers

*"In the journal I do not just express myself more openly than I could to any person; I create myself."* - Susan Sontag

*"I don't journal to 'be productive'...The pages aren't intended for anyone but me. It's the most cost-effective therapy I've ever found."* - Tim Ferriss

*"I write entirely to find out what I'm thinking, what I'm looking at, what I see and what it means. What I want and what I fear."* - Joan Didion

*"...there are a thousand thoughts lying within a man that he does not know till he takes up the pen to write."* - William Makepeace Thackeray

*"I can shake off everything as I write: my sorrows disappear, my courage is reborn."* - Anne Frank

*"It was always intimidating starting a new journal. So much pressure to make everything perfect from the start. It was a relief each time she made her first mistake or two and realized that her journal was more gracious and forgiving toward her than she was toward herself."* - Alana Terry

*"Why one writes is a question I can answer easily, having so often asked it of myself. I believe one writes because one has to create a world in which one can live. I could not live in any of the worlds offered to me — the world of my parents, the world of war, the world of politics. I had to create a world of my own, like a climate, a country, an atmosphere in which I could breathe, reign, and recreate myself when destroyed by living. That, I believe, is the reason for every work of art."* - Anaïs Nin

# 4. RELEASE

Release definition: *"to set free from restraint, confinement, or servitude; to relieve from something that confines, burdens or oppresses."* - Merriam-Webster

B EFORE REBOOTING A computer we are usually advised to "uninstall" any programs suspected of having been corrupted. If you were in a cult or abusive family you probably had a limited, biased, controlling, – *corrupt* – operating system 'installed' through the process of indoctrination.

When you walk away you may assume that you have "refreshed" your belief system and are ready to start anew. After a few years, however, you may find you have not cleaned out all the old, contaminated files. You may have done work on healing and recovering, but still find yourself stalling or crashing unexpectedly due to lingering mental and emotional malware.

Before installing a 'new operating system' or adding new files about how to move forward with life, you need to first release the old programs, beliefs, points of view, assumptions, mental maps, and habits that keep you insidiously bound to a faulty 'reality' that literally doesn't work in the realm of freedom. You need to switch off any outdated narrative (operating system) about what your life is about now and what you are capable of now.

The point of reviewing and re-assessing your story, recommended in the last chapter, is to help make what is still unconscious about your operating system conscious. Then you will know what files to delete and what new programs, of your choosing, will help you move forward with life. Once you lay down the burdens and baggage of the past, you can move forward unencumbered into the future.

Based on your review and re-assessment in the last chapter you should have a good idea of what you still need to cut away and what parts of yourself may have been ignored, suppressed or left behind and need to be reactivated and embraced. If you were taught that everything about the world is evil, that the world is bound for imminent destruction, that a promised land is on the horizon, that only a future paradise has value, that you would live forever only if you were obedient, and that anything in the here-and-now has no value ... there is a lot to cut away!

Perhaps you have already released most of the corrupt files and your review and reassessment revealed some remaining hidden pockets of old habits, defenses, guilt, or shame that are holding you back. Be alert as well for the discovery of sweet pieces of your repressed self that are calling to be recognized and re-incorporated back into your life. There are not only things to release, but there is much to reclaim. This can be an exciting and invigorating process.

Occasionally, instead of being excited about recovering our authentic self we can get stuck as armchair critics caught in bitterness, victimhood, and occasional tirades of judgment and wishes for revenge. Such attitudes do not serve our health nor facilitate our ability to move ahead.

Teacher and author Charles Eisenstein says we must:

*"...remove the disorienting fog of habits and beliefs, left-overs of the old paradigms that obscure our internal guidance system."*

You do not want to find yourself just re-arranging the old beliefs in your mind. You must consciously release them and replace them.

As well, without realizing it we become attached to our suffering. Twentieth Century Philosopher George Gurdjieff warns, *"A man will renounce any pleasures you like but he will not give up his suffering."* How attached are you to your suffering? Is attachment to unfair victimization what is now keeping you stuck?

Releasing old, outdated ways and beliefs does not occur with the tap of a magic wand. It requires on-going, active observation of the way you think and act. When you notice yourself caught in an old perception or habit, it requires you then say *"No"* to yourself and substitute a thought or behavior that would better serve you and your goals now.

## THE INNER CRITIC

One of the main things we have to cut out of our lives is the inner critic which was installed in place by the abusive system. This is the demanding, inner voice that finds fault with our behaviours, ideas, new goals, and our very self. There are few things that will stall our movement forward in life more than on-going self-judgment and self-criticism. Criticism constricts, constrains, and restrains. Many therapists still use the word Freud coined for the hyper-critical component of the self – the *"superego"*. It is the judgmental, parent-like, sometimes harsh and punitive voice that is always there telling us we are not good enough. See Chapter 5 and Chapter 10 for a more detailed description of the superego and how its harsh aspect can keep you stuck.

You can also think of one of the tasks to get unstuck as decreasing clutter – the clutter in your mind, the clutter of the inner critic/

super-ego's judgments, the clutter of old beliefs, the clutter of certain habits and routines, the clutter of limiting assumptions about what is possible for you, and the clutter of old roles you mistakenly believe you must continue to play.

About ten years ago, despite the warnings and mocking of my inner critic, I took up a new pastime - painting. As I developed techniques as a painter I discovered it is often what I *remove* from the canvas that produces the effect I want. Let me tell you a bit about this discovery:

Several years ago, in an effort to get all my painting, collaging, and journal-making materials off of the island in our kitchen, my husband built an art studio in a section of our garage. (I make mainly abstract art with acrylic paint on large canvases and craft handmade journals.) In abstract painting I love textures and like to apply layers of transparent paint that allow the history of layers beneath to peek through.

I soon discovered that beautiful effects can be created by *removing* parts of the paint already added — by scraping, sanding, wiping, scratching, etc. It turns out to be a process of adding *and subtracting*. However, it's almost always after subtracting some of the layers that the painting I am looking for reveals itself. The act of removal more often than not produces exactly what I had been trying to get by adding more paint. Painter Pablo Picasso said, "*Art is the elimination of the unnecessary.*"

I have also learned to be willing to eliminate seemingly 'precious' areas I feel attached to on the canvas. In life, as in art, often what we remove, what we let go of, what we cut away, what we are willing to release, becomes pivotal in creating the space for the *piece de resistance* to emerge. I soon discovered and now use multiple ways of removing paint and eliminating previous strokes.

A great piece of art, a well-edited book, a clothing ensemble, a well-decorated room, and a good life are, counterintuitively, often improved by what is removed or released. One of the first things I worked to release in life was my inner critic.

## QUESTIONS TO HELP ASSESS WHAT NEEDS TO BE REMOVED OR RELEASED:

111. What might you need to remove or subtract from your life now?

112. What habitual distractions might you need to replace with new activities?

113. Have you been able to release past hurts and disappointments? Explain.

114. Did you take time to "marinate in" the freedom and relief of releasing parts of the past?

115. What pieces of the past do you still carry that are preventing you from moving on?

116. What distorted thinking about your capabilities and competencies needs to be subtracted?

117. How might you not be telling the truth to yourself?

118. How might you be contributing to keeping yourself stuck?

119. What fears do you need to expose and eliminate?

120. What ego defenses against those fears might be holding you back? (Ego defenses such as: denial, avoidance, projection, rationalization, repression, etc.)

121. How can you begin to work now to let go of these ego defenses?

122. What else or who else might be contributing to blocking your progress?

123. Are there limits you have unconsciously placed on what is possible for you?

124. Do you have unrealistic expectations of being able to create a 'perfect' world for yourself?

125. Do you still have to release the fantasy of a utopian paradise where everything will play out with perfection and learn instead to deal with the reality of what is possible?

126. Do you realize the limits you have placed on your life affect

what you are able to notice, what information you absorb, what choices you make, what risks you feel able to take?

127. How do you construct beliefs around your fears and then perceive them to be true – when, in fact, they are not?

128. What fear-based beliefs are no longer serving you and need to be released?

129. What current emotional and/or life burdens do you need to unload?

130. If you have trouble finding the energy to move forward beyond what is blocking you, what could be blocking your energy?

131. How might unresolved anger be blocking you from moving forward?

132. If it is not anger at others that is keeping you stuck, could it be anger at yourself?

133. Do you think it is possible to move freely forward with your life if you are not self-accepting?

134. What do you need to forgive yourself for, in order to enjoy more self-acceptance?

135. How might you be consumed by wanting to prove everyone who hurt you wrong?

136. Are you attached to things or people that are hurting you or pulling you down?

137. Do you, at a deep level, believe you are unlovable and therefore unworthy?

138. Did a part of you, long ago, decide there were intractable limits on what was available to you – on how far you could go?

139. How long will you continue to live with these erroneous beliefs about limits?

140. How can you replace what holds you down with dreams and goals that excite you?

141. How can you dig deep and find what motivates and exhilarates you now?

142. Are you stuck because you have not allowed yourself to discover your passion, your talents, your genius, or your special area of competence?

143. Is it possible you are not stuck, but stalling because of fear of failure?

144. How would you move forward if you did not fear failing?

145. Looking back on past 'failures', can you mine them now for the strengths acquired?

If you are in denial about old cult programming and any harsh interdictions still rattling around in your body/mind, or of the wounds they cause, you will remain stuck. You have to make a point of releasing all the old indoctrination, limitations, prohibitions, and counter-productive behaviors sourced in a cult or in an abusive past. You have to let go of the old, corrupt operating system and reboot with a new operating system of your choosing. For the moment, concentrate on closing down the old operating system (including the voice of the inner critic) and each and every corrupt file you can find that was created by internalizing faulty family or cult concepts.

## MORE QUESTIONS ABOUT WHAT YOU MAY STILL NEED TO RELEASE:

146. Where is it you still continue to hold on, instead of letting go?

147. Are you caught in the religious teaching that you are a sinner, fundamentally flawed, and in need of redemption?

148. How might this belief keep you stuck?

149. Do you realize there is another unconscious belief married to that one – one that says as a sinner you are never good enough, are condemned to toil, to suffer, and required to atone?

150. Are you unconsciously attached to the suffering this belief causes and resistant to let it go?

151. How can you help yourself release the old beliefs used by religion and parents to control you and now embrace the unique trajectory of your new, free life?

152. Because of suffering and shame, how might you be hiding from the life you long to enjoy?

153. How can you let go of the fear-based or shame-based habit of isolating or hiding?

154. What people, situations, habits or beliefs are keeping you stuck, or drained of the energy needed to move forward? How can let go of those things/people?

155. How do you generally spend the 24 hours you have in each day?

156. What parts of your current routine are no longer serving you and need to be eliminated?

157. Are you engaged in self-criticism that undermines your ability to get unstuck?

158. Is there some part of you that believes criticizing yourself will motivate you to action?

159. Can you challenge those self-criticisms and release them?

160. Because of the cult teaching of eternal life on a paradise earth, did you come to believe you had all the time in the world to accomplish your goals?

161. Have you come to terms with the limited time you have on this planet and that you need to skillfully manage your time in order to accomplish your goals?

162. Is it time to "refresh" by shutting down the operating system keeping you tied to the cult?

163. How can you fully mine any setbacks or 'failures' for learnings and strengths imparted, before you let them go?

164. Do you have unreasonable expectations of yourself that you need to release? Describe.

165. How can you begin to allow yourself new experiences outside

of the confines of your current story (for example: "*the cult took everything from me*" or "*the abuse ruined my life*")?

When I consider question #154 above, I think of an example of my own where I had to let go of a decent relationship that was draining my energies and interfering with personal and professional goals. Because this person seemed like a friend and had, in fact, done many seemingly thoughtful things during the friendship it was difficult to see and accept that I was being unduly influenced to further *their* goals. Yes, they were goals I admired, but it seemed I had to learn the hard way that undue influence is not only used for criminal or immoral purposes. Undue influence and manipulation, even for worthy goals, is still exploitative. So I decided to let go of a relationship that pleased me on some levels because it consistently siphoned my time and energy away from my own projects with frequent requests that I contribute my competencies to theirs.

We all occasionally – especially when we feel stuck – have to take stock of the relationships and situations we are in and determine whether they are in any way controlling, manipulative, exploitative or psychologically, emotionally or physically draining. Sometimes when we feel unable to move forward it is because of external forces claiming our energies and diverting us from our own projects. If that is the case, we have to be willing to work with the person to weed out the maladaptive behaviors or, when that doesn't work, release the relationship altogether.

Another thing that helps with a post trauma recovery reboot is to let go of our resistance to experiencing pain or discomfort, and our resistance to the unavoidable anxiety produced by change. Satish Kumar in his book "*The Buddha and the Terrorist*" tells us:

"*... pain is part of life. By accepting it, its intensity is reduced. Do not resist it. Resistance to pain brings tension and anxiety, anxiety leads to fear. Fear of pain is worse than pain itself. This pain will pass.*"

Release your resistance to experiencing discomfort as you work toward change. Letting go, by the way, is not a onetime event – it is something that must be done again and again over a lifetime.

166. Are there people, situations or things from which you need to walk away in order to reclaim the time and energy you need to move forward with your life?

167. Is there an inner critic walking through life with you that you need to restrain or release?

## Quotations to Inspire You About the Need to Release:

*"One of the hardest lessons in life is letting go. Whether it's guilt, anger, love, loss, or betrayal. Change is never easy. We fight to hold on and we fight to let go."* - Amy Brucker

*"Ego, which wants to keep everything familiar, is terrified of losing itself, not to mention the old patterns and conditioned habits that prop it up."* - Timothy Butler

*"Freud taught us that it wasn't God that imposed judgment on us and made us feel guilty when we stepped out of line. Instead, it was the superego – that idealized concept of what a good person is supposed to be and do – given to us by our parents, that condemned us for what had been hitherto regarded as ungodly behavior."* - Tony Campolo, sociologist and author

*"Development involves giving up a smaller story in order to wake up to a larger story."* - Jean Houston

*"It is frightening to lose the old structures of security, but you will find that even as you might lose things that were unthinkable to lose, you will be okay ... Possibilities that didn't even exist in the old story lie before you, even if you have no idea how to get there."* - Charles Eisenstein

*"In the process of letting go, you will lose many things from the past, but you will find yourself."* - Deepak Chopra

*"The greatest need of our time is to clean out the enormous mass of mental and emotional rubbish that clutters our minds and makes of all*

*political and social life a mass illness. Without this housecleaning, we cannot begin to see. Unless we see, we cannot think."* - Thomas Merton

*"Reject your sense of injury and the injury itself disappears."* - Marcus Aurelius

*"Getting over a painful experience is much like crossing monkey bars. You have to let go at some point in order to move forward."* - C.S. Lewis

*"The difficulty lies not so much in developing new ideas as in escaping from old ones."* - John Maynard Keynes

*"The truth is, unless you let go, unless you forgive yourself, unless you forgive the situation, unless you realize that the situation is over, you cannot move forward."* - Steve Maraboli

*"We need to forgive the fact that we're stuck and begin to be willing to investigate what's underneath our behaviors."* - Tara Brach

*"Gentle me ...*
*into an unclenched moment,*
*a deep breath*
*a letting go*
*of heavy experiences*
*of shriveling anxieties*
*of dead certainties ..."*

- Ted Loder

*"let it go – the*
*smashed word broken*
*open vow or*
*the oath cracked length*
*wise – let it go it*
*was sworn to*
*go*

*let them go – the*
*truthful liars and*
*the false fair friends*
*and the boths and*
*neithers – you must let them go they*
*were born*
*to go*

*let all go – the*
*big small middling*
*tall bigger really*
*the biggest and all*
*things – let all go*
*dear*

*so comes love"*

- e.e. cummings

# 5. RECOGNIZE & REASSESS

Recognize definition: *"...to acknowledge de facto existence...of; to perceive to be something or someone previously known; to perceive clearly."* Re-assess definition: *"to re-determine the importance ... or value of."* - Merriam-Webster

ONE QUESTION WE ask ourselves once out of an oppressive situation is, *"who am I now?"* In effect, even though we chose to leave, we have lost a piece of our identity. The good news is your identity as a victim of control, trauma or abuse was only a part of who you are. You were always, and are now, so much more than that.

Part of your work now is to identify the mind-sets, parts, and personas you use to function in the world and to make sure none of them continue to be trauma-driven, cult-based, or counterproductive. We all have many personas or roles we use throughout any given day – e.g. the manager, the parent, the fixer, the consoler, the joker, the thinker, the helper, the skeptic, etc.

The bad news is that to survive in an oppressive family or group most of us had to hide or bury away our authentic self. We must now let that core part of ourselves know it is safe to re-emerge and take its rightful place in our life. We want to reawaken and welcome our true self. This chapter will provide life hacks to help you recognize and reassess unhelpful personas or parts, and to reclaim and embrace your authentic self.

I once read the deepest spiritual wound is *"the wound of not being allowed to be one's self"*. What phrase could more aptly describe one of the main abuses that occur in coercive control situations – not being allowed to be yourself?

Once out, our job is to not only grieve the losses, heal the wounds, and engage with our new life, but also to reawaken our authentic self. We quickly realize, for example, we are no longer who we were in the coercive environment. But we have yet to connect with who we truly are apart from it. It is essential to recognize and reclaim your true self – the self you know will reflect your core values and help you find your true purpose. The next chapter will help you get in touch with core values.

It can be challenging to coax the authentic self out of hiding. It's a common struggle, this quest to become one's authentic self. Finding and becoming who we really are is a task that takes time and we must be patient with the process. Selected phrases from poet, Derek Walcott's (1930-2017), poem "Love After Love" describes the moment of finally welcoming one's authentic self:

> *"The time will come*
> *when, with elation*
> *you will greet yourself arriving*
> *at your own door, in your own mirror*
> *and each will smile at the other's welcome ...*
> *You will love again the stranger who was your self ...*
> *the stranger who has loved you*
> *all your life, whom you ignored ...*
> *who knows you by heart ... "*

In the cult in which I was raised we were literally told to take off the *"old personality"* and put on their *"new personality"*. Their narrowly defined *"new personality"* left masses of us walking around like robots programmed to believe the same doctrines, perceive things in the same way, and to behave in the same pre-packaged ways. How can one live life fully when one is alienated from their authentic self – when living via parts or personas that pleased our abusers?

Even once out of the traumatic environment, those old robotic ways of being may show up as our default ways of operating in the world – to our detriment. To "*put on the new personality*" we had to repress our authentic self, and that forced repression is not quickly undone. It takes some serious reassessment and recalibration of who we are. We have to discover what compensatory roles or personas we habitually assume – what mindsets are holding us down – in order to finally divest ourselves of conditioned, inauthentic selves.

## RECOGNIZING THE AUTHENTIC SELF & DISCRIMINATING IT FROM DEFENSIVE SELVES

In order to leave the group and then cope with the aftermath of leaving we may develop protective patterns/personas to survive – before we even have time to unearth our authentic self. Without realizing it, we can then become identified with these protective patterns (mind-sets, ego-states, personas or defenses) and begin to feel stuck, not realizing it is the protective pattern (persona or part) itself that is keeping us stuck.

We cannot successfully move forward with life while in a defensive or protective stance that unconsciously activates the fight, flight or freeze functions of the autonomic nervous system. Those should be temporary stances, measures, functions, parts, and/or personas that help us cope through crisis, not permanent postures or attitudes with which to move through life.

Life is complex – especially when we give up a world view and lose our sense of belonging. To cope with such complexity we often, and understandably, assume roles or personas.

In the midst of crisis, while coping with trauma we may assume other roles or stances due to our situation. Because of adverse circumstances we may have taken on personas such as: *the secretive one, the submissive one, the people-pleaser, the minimizer, the avoider, the ever-cheerful-one, the hard worker, the depressed one, the dependent one, the angry one, the bully, the poor-me one,* etc.

We each need to take a deep look at the defensive, protective *roles, ego-states, personas or subpersonalities* we operate from on a day-to-day basis, and take responsibility to decide whether those personas or roles are still required once the worst of the crisis is over.

Richard C. Schwartz, Ph.D., LMFT describing his Internal Family Systems Model in his book, "*Introduction to the Internal Family Systems Model*" shares a long list of "c" words which describe people when their authentic self has been buried and false selves have been constructed in order to survive. These false selves could be described with Schwartz's list of "c" words: "*closed, confused, clouded, clogged, congested, chaotic, cowardly, cautious, compliant, complacent, conceited, computer-like, critical, confronting, craving, cruel, cynical, contemptuous, controlling, coercive, commanding, cocky, compulsive, colluding, conquesting, crafty, clever, and crazy.*"

168.   Do any of those words describe you or your personas/parts? Describe them and how they play out in your life.

Once we become aware we are using these attitudes or ways of being to protect our buried authentic self, we need to thank the part/persona for the role it has played in defending us and then slowly and respectfully begin the process of dis-identifying from it. We could also call this dis-identification process a *mindset intervention* – or an ego-state reboot.

It could be as you proceed with this exploration of your inner parts or personas that you discover a part that is **self-hating** or self-rejecting. This part needs to be acknowledged and given an opportunity to express its needs and fears (use your journal for this). This part does not need to be condemned but needs to be acknowledged for even its maladaptive way of trying to protect you from taking risks. *However,* you do not want to live your life from this stance and must learn to dis-identify from this part. This would best be done with the help of a licensed psychotherapist who is familiar with the Internal Family Systems Model or with the Roberto Assagioli (Psychosynthesis) concept of sub-personalities and dis-identification from them.

Novelist and essayist Anaïs Nin describes our complex, multi-faceted inner lives in this way: *"We do not grow absolutely, chronologically. We grow sometimes in one dimension, and not in another; unevenly. We grow partially. We are relative. We are mature in one realm, childish in another. The past, present, and future mingle and pull us backward, forward, or fix us in the present. We are made up of layers, cells, constellations."* The Diary of Anais Nin, Vol.4

## SOME DEFENSIVE SELVES WE NEED TO RECOGNIZE & RE-ASSESS

There are other less extreme ego states, parts or personas that we can work with on our own. For example, in order to leave a cult you had to become clear about what you disagreed with, what you opposed. As the cult or oppressive family bombarded you with reasons why you should stop thinking independently and conform, perhaps to survive and to stand up for yourself you assumed a stance of opposing – or being "oppositional" – even if it was only in your own mind.

It is understandable that one would oppose all the demands to conform and bury one's true self. So perhaps to muster the courage to leave and to justify the decision to leave you had to assume a persona that could now be described as **oppositional**. You had to oppose the beliefs and controls in order to escape. However now free, does an oppositional stance in life help or hurt you?

In a general sense, a person who is habitually oppositional will just go on automatic pilot and disagree with almost everything anyone says or suggests. While that may have been a necessary stance to help you leave a way of life that was so controlling, it may not serve your current desire to move ahead with your life. You may now need a life hack to let go of, or dis-identify from, that oppositional persona. Don't worry, you will not forget how to speak up when you don't agree with something. You just won't feel compelled to oppose everything, all the time, once you are no longer identified with it.

Being oppositional is a stance that consumes tremendous energy and does not engender much compassion or support from those around you. There are other more reasonable, authentic and skillful ways to respond to what you do not agree with and make your movement forward in life easier.

Another possible persona or ego-state we can get stuck in is the **know-it-all** persona or mind-set. For example, based on what you were taught in a cult and all you were told about Biblical prophecies, the present condition of, and the future of the world, etc., perhaps you developed a *know-it-all persona* – without even realizing it. Now, as you step into your new life, it will serve you well to drop a "*know-it-all*" persona.

A better stance while creating a new life is to be curious, ready to share your competencies where you can. An open, curious stance or mind-set will make you much more welcome in the new environments in which you find yourself.

Another sub-personality we often carry with us is the **complaining/critical** one. Perhaps we were taught to judge whether others were living up to the standards of a cult or our family. We were taught to be critical of the behaviors of people "in the world". We now have to take responsibility to examine whether we inadvertently slip into a judgmental or critical persona. The path ahead of you will be easier if you can dis-identify from, or drop this persona.

This does not mean you now have to allow everything, or adopt a **walk-all-over-me** persona. You will not lose your ability to make judgments about what is right or wrong for you, or to use critical thinking to discriminate between options. You just don't want to bring the negative energy of a critical, judgmental persona into your interactions to build a new life – nor do you want to live from the other passive extreme.

Perhaps you assumed personas or roles to please others or to hide parts of yourself that you thought were unacceptable. We might call that a **people-pleasing** persona. It is now your privilege to respond honestly to people who expect you to always accommodate them.

Step out of any people-pleasing role by simply saying, "*I prefer to do it this way*". This will be a wonderful act of self-affirmation. You can now drop the persona developed to please, conform and compensate for your trauma-imposed insecurities.

Many who feel stuck and unable to move ahead are struggling with a **saboteur** persona that keeps them fumbling, scrambling, procrastinating, messing up, having accidents, getting sick, etc. To move ahead with your life you have to get to know the *inner saboteur* and find out what it is afraid of – what it fears would happen if you were to move ahead with your life – why it is trying to keep you stuck exactly where you are? As we will discuss in Chapter 10, it is perhaps linked to the "superego" trying to protect, distract, or punish you – and is sabotaging any efforts to create a new post-trauma life.

Are you caught in a **victim** *sub-personality* since realizing how much you were deceived and exploited by a cult or mistreated and abused in a domestic situation? To move forward with your life, you cannot forever respond to life as a victim. We all spend a period of time nursing wounds after being victimized by deception, manipulation and exploitation. We *were* victimized, but how long will we remain their victim? Just know the victim stance can either immobilize you or keep you stuck in rage and even in aggressive, oppositional behaviors.

The healthy goal is to move beyond the personas of victim and even the identity of survivor. Both, in their own way, keep you tied to the past – and that keeps you stuck. There are many other mindsets and roles that do not help us move forward with our life. Try to recognize the ones you habitually use and reassess whether you want to operate from them. If not, you will want to learn the following life hacks on how to dis-identify from ego-states or personas.

## RECOGNIZING & WELCOMING THE QUALITIES OF THE AUTHENTIC SELF

There may be some of the old personas that are still useful to you, that help you cope and adapt, and that don't keep you stuck. Take responsibility to examine the personas you habitually use and ask yourself if they help or hurt you. Drop the ones you don't need and be aware of and support the ones you do. Then use them in a way that does not crowd out or bury your real Self. Give support and affirmation to the personas, parts, mind-sets, qualities you know will help you embrace your new free life. Withdraw inner/outer resources and support from the less-adaptive personas you developed to survive any control or abuse. We all respond best to life when in a **grounded, mindful adult stance** that reflects our authentic self, rather than in a persona developed in response to deception, abuse, control, and exploitation.

As well as assuming responsibility for the trauma-related personas (the defensive, false, protective, maladaptive selves) you now need to drop, you will need to look at new roles and personas you want to take on that will help you live more authentically, freely, and fully. Most importantly, you must take responsibility for finding and being your authentic, real self.

Dr. Schwartz, in his observation of clients that were able to step into their "real" self while working in therapy, noticed these clients often embodied the following positive, "c" word qualities: "*calmness, clarity, curiosity, compassion, confidence, courage, creativity, connectedness … consciousness, contentedness, constancy …*"

168a.  Do you recognize any of these healthy qualities that you are already manifesting in your life – the courageous one, the confident one, the curious one, the calm one, etc.? Describe how they play out and help in your life.

All of these more authentic parts of yourself are waiting to work for you as you claim and chart your new life.

## LIFE HACKS TO DIS-IDENTIFY FROM A PERSONA, PART, or EGO-STATE

To disrupt and dis-identify from a maladaptive part or persona, the first things you have to do are:

- become aware of it – recognize it – reassess whether it serves you or not
- observe it – it's postures, it behaviors, the typical thoughts you think as 'it'
- discern the need it fulfills for you – and when it usually makes an appearance
- sit with the part and see what it may be trying to tell you – what it is trying to do
- give it a descriptive name, if you like
- thank it for how it has tried to 'help' you, and tell it you now no longer need it
- remind yourself that there is more to you than this part, this mood, this mind-set, this way of being, this identification
- disrupt its pattern even further by shifting your posture, stretching, taking deep cleansing breaths, imagining the part or mind-set exiting with each exhalation
- turn your attention to a mind-set that supports your well-being and breathe in the positive qualities of the persona you select, e.g. your confident, centered part

These actions or disruptions act as a powerful intervention to dis-identify from old, once protective but now counterproductive patterns. To "dis-identify" from an ego-state is to release yourself from its grip, to make a shift out of its limited perspective, to step out of a negative mood or way of being, to not be enveloped or dominated by a defensive character trait that keeps you stuck in old patterns.

Usually personas develop in order to protect us. Sometimes they are not up-to-date with our changing circumstances and need to be thanked for their service, but informed that their services are no longer needed and are, in fact, now getting in the way and keeping us stuck. This disrupting of a pattern by observing it and communicating with it should be done with compassion.

Again, to dis-identify from a maladaptive persona you need to become aware of the body sensations, emotions, thought patterns, behaviors and postures that indicate you are caught in it (e.g. a wounded or angry or paralyzed self). Give the mind-set or role a name and become familiar with what triggers its appearance. Does it appear when you are tired, stressed, lonely, anxious, when you try to step out of your comfort zone, or when you break a coercive control group rule? Look for things you do or think that consistently signal an identification with a certain sub-personality.

As said, I use deep cleansing breaths, make an effort to straighten my spine, and remind myself I am, for example no longer an abandoned child, but now a competent adult who no longer needs to feel sorry for herself. You can do the same as a hack to dis-identify from any of your debilitating personas. Awareness, grounded feet, conscious breathing and the intent to make the shift are private yet powerful adjustments you can make to dis-identify from ego-states that hold you down.

Remind yourself that while you may have, for example, a self-pitying or victim mind-set/persona, it is not your true self. Try to shift your awareness and stance into the grounded, authentic adult you are now and continue your day supporting that more adaptive, healthy stance.

While assuming responsibility for any trauma-related personas (the false, protective, maladaptive selves) that you now need to drop, you will want to look at new roles and personas you can take on that will help you live more authentically, independently, freely, and fully – such as *the calm one, the courageous one, the curious one, the grateful one, the resourceful one*, etc..

Most importantly, you must now take responsibility for finding, supporting and being *your authentic, adult self* – most of the time. This is the 'true you' identification that will help you move past old limitations, live more in alignment with your true values, and reach your goals.

You don't have to drop or eliminate every one of your personas, sub-personalities. You don't have to chastise yourself when you notice yourself caught in one. There may be some that have adaptive, useful qualities that don't keep you stuck. Take responsibility to examine and reassess the personas you habitually use and ask yourself if they are helpful or hurtful. Drop the ones that are hurting you or holding you back. Be aware of the ones you do use – and use them in a way that does not hide, crowd out, or hinder the real you.

To repeat, the life hack is to give inner support to the adaptive, resilient, adult personas you know will help you embrace your new free life. You want to live from an ego-state that is able to deal with reality as it presents itself and does not have the limited, child-like perspectives of many of your more defensive (yet maladaptive) ego-states.

Withdraw inner resources and support from the personas you developed to survive in a cult or an abusive family and that are holding you back now with their limited views. We all respond best to life when in a grounded adult stance rather than in an immature ego-state. Dis-identification may feel a little awkward at first, but as you use it, it will become second nature to you – like taking off a sweater when you feel too hot.

There is a Native American story about a grandfather who says he has two wolves fighting in his heart – one who is angry and vengeful, and the other who is compassionate and loving. Asked which wolf (persona) will win the fight inside his heart, he replies, "*The one I feed*".

So too, for each of us. The personas that will dominate our life – the personas or parts that will help us get unstuck – are the ones we support with our inner resources of attention, support, care, and kindness. Which ego-states do you "*feed*"?

Below are a few examples of statements or affirmations to help you dis-identify from particular mind-sets, parts, attitudes toward life, powerful feelings, child ego-states, etc. You can adapt any (by inserting the particular persona, feeling, mood, ego-state, etc. that applies in your case and adjust the wording, as needed, to the way you would express yourself) of the following phrases to your own ego-states.

1. *"While I notice myself occasionally caught in a **victim** persona, I know that I, my true, grounded, adult self, am not a victim. I now release all victim-like thinking and feelings. I choose to identify with, and act from, the part of me that is an independent free agent, able to problem-solve, and cope with the magnificent but sometimes unpredictable process of life."*

2. *"While I may feel burdened, even stuck, in beliefs, personality traits, and/or behaviors learned in a coercive environment, I know that I, my true self, am so much more than that '**brainwashed**' persona. I choose to identify with my authentic, objective self with its values, worldview, preferences and feelings."*

3. *"While I may have dragged a **shy** persona along with me from my childhood, I know that I, my true self, am not only a shy person. I choose to relax into life and release all feelings of inferiority, and fear of taking my place in the world. I choose to identify with the part of me that is comfortable in my skin and comfortable expressing my opinions, needs, and preferences."*

4. *"While I may catch myself in acts of **self-sabotage**, I know that I, my true self am not a saboteur and do not deserve punishment or thwarted goals due to unconsciously-orchestrated mistakes, failure, depression, accidents, illness, etc. I relax and release myself from any negative tendency to distract or punish myself for exercising my right to be who I am. I affirm my right to make decisions and take risks to act on my own behalf."*

5.  *"While I may have a part that is **angry** about all that was sto-len from me by a cult or abusive family, I know that I, my true self, am not only an angry person. I choose to acknowledge any anger that may be there but not identify with it and not act from it. I direct the energies of any justifiable anger into positive projects that make up for the losses experienced. I may experience anger, but I myself am not anger, and I do not have to be identified with the anger. It helps when I say "I am experiencing anger moving through my body/mind", rather than "I am angry"."*

6.  *"While there may be a part of me that feels **guilty** about leaving the coercive control group, its god, and my family and friends who continue to conform, I know the guilt is just energy passing through me and is not the real me. I refuse to say "I am guilty", for I, my true self, am guilty of nothing for leaving. I identify with my authentic self who has the right to dream, explore, discover, choose, and act on my own behalf. I relax into life as a human who makes mistakes, just like all other humans. I try to fix any mistakes and I forgive myself where I can't. I release feelings of guilt. I embrace my free-dom, minus any demoralizing drag of guilt."*

7.  *"While I notice I can get caught in feelings of **discourage-ment and doubt**, I know that I, my true self, am so much more than that. I lovingly release all feelings of discourage-ment, hopelessness, and helplessness. I use deep cleansing breathes to dis-identify from any discouraged persona now."*

8.  *"While I sometimes catch myself believing I am **unlovable**, I know that I, my true self, am lovable, good, and enough. I lovingly release the old, erroneous belief that I am unlovable and the persona that acts as if I am unlovable. I choose to identify and act from my authentic self which has always been lovable whether those around me acknowledged my lovability or not."*

9. *"While I can easily find myself caught up in waves of **anxiety** and can to begin act like, and refer to myself as, "an anxious person", I know that I, my true self, am not only anxious. I lovingly relax and release the waves of anxiety that occasionally go through my body/mind, and identify with my authentic, grounded, comfortable adult self."*

10. *"While I can occasionally find myself in a mind-set that tries to **control** everything (probably because I had so little control over anything while in my dysfunctional family or in a cult), I know I am much more than that controlling persona. I am learning when I operate from my authentic self I have nothing to prove, nothing to manage, no one to save, and can allow life to unfold as it will – knowing I can handle problems or feelings as they arise. I am working to dis-identify from a controlling part and identify with my competent, calm, accepting Self."*

Did you notice the above statements help you to relate TO feelings, thoughts, parts, or mind-sets, rather than to relate FROM them? Did you notice the relief you experience when you move toward identification with your authentic, grounded, adult Self? The relief can be palpable.

When we relate to life and circumstances FROM a particular persona, thought or feeling, we are identified with it, enveloped by it, unable to see any other perspective, stuck in a crippling pattern with limited, if any, choices (e.g. FROM: *"I will never recover from being rejected and abandoned by my family – my life is ruined."*).

When we relate TO the circumstance (e.g. TO: *"Yes I have been abandoned by family and friends, but I am determined to build a new life with people whose love is not conditional. I can do this!"* or *"Yes, I am experiencing old fear learned in the past, but I will not let it determine how I move through my day."*) we recognize the state or mind-set but are not trapped in (identified) and governed by the state, feeling, or thought. What freedom!

Please do the work necessary to adopt the habit of relating TO your thoughts and feelings rather than FROM them. This is a powerful life hack. Again, relate TO any maladaptive thoughts and feelings, not FROM them!

> *"I am larger and better than I thought.*
> *I did not think I held so much goodness."*
>
> \- Walt Whitman

## Quotations to Help Recognize & Reassess Mindsets, Ego States, or Personas:

*"Maybe the journey isn't so much about becoming anything. Maybe it's about un-becoming everything that isn't really you, so you can be who you were meant to be in the first place."* - Paulo Coelho

*"... the single most vital step on your journey toward enlightenment is this: learn to dis-identify from your mind."* - Eckhart Tolle

*"Do I contradict myself? Very well then, I contradict myself. (I am large, I contain multitudes.)"* - Walt Whitman

*"Addressing different sub-personalities is a really wonderful way to help people develop a profound acceptance of their full experience ... It's about working with the parts of ourselves that aren't so noble and opening up to them – accepting and exploring them."* - Ron Siegel, Psy.D.

*"When you see those selves ... you can make friends with them – accept that they're all you – and then make choices about which self you want to strengthen."* - Kelly McGonigal, Ph.D.

*"Our persona was not created by accident; it was created in order to camouflage the parts of ourselves we deemed the most undesirable and to overcompensate for what we believed to be our deepest flaws."* - Debbie Ford

*"When you become a slave to a public persona and don't feel comfortable without it, it becomes a shield, but it shouldn't come at the expense of your self-worth."* - Gugu Mbatha-Raw

*"Knowing others is wisdom, knowing yourself is enlightenment."* - Lao Tzu

*"To the extent that you actually realize that you are not, for example, your anxieties, then your anxieties no longer threaten you. Even if anxiety is present, it no longer overwhelms you because you are no longer exclusively tied to it. You are no longer courting it, fighting it, resisting it, or running from it. In the most radical fashion, anxiety is thoroughly accepted as it is and allowed to move as it will...you are simply watching it pass by."* - Ken Wilber

# 6. RESTORE

Restore definition: "*...bring back, reinstate, re-establish, return something to a former position, or place.*" Merriam-Webster

A FTER LEAVING A high-control community there is a lot we have to release as discussed in previous chapters. Sometimes however, we forget there are important things we need to restore.

If you were in a controlling environment you were probably told what to believe, how to think, how to behave and, implicitly, what to feel. That meant you had to suppress your own thoughts, feelings, and desires. You had to suppress the natural human inclination to consider options, to entertain new ideas, to be curious, to explore, to experiment and to discover. This, as said earlier, is the critical spiritual wound – not being able to be yourself.

It would be easy to assume that once away from the influence of the invasive group, your authentic self would automatically re-emerge. However we can accelerate the process of restoring our real self by devoting time to compassionately coaxing it out of hiding. We want to restore our authentic self to its rightful place. "*Our minds become reactive, and we feel estranged from ourselves as a result; locked out of our own houses, we are in need of the key to return.*" - Mark Epstein, M.D.

Part of that coaxing requires you to reassure your authentic self it is now safe to come forth – to come home – and express itself and its values. Tell your true self it no longer has to live as if the group's lies are true. It no longer has to hide its truth, its preferences, and its deepest longings. Let's look at some of the keys to restoring your authentic self to its rightful place.

Perhaps you wonder exactly what your real self wants and needs. This is where explorative writing can be a great help. In your journal you can ask yourself the questions provided here and test out the answers that will reveal what *you* value – what *you* want – what *you* need – what *you* are willing to work to attain. Doing this may help you better determine your current life purpose.

You can view this self-restoration work as a burden or as a privilege. Ask yourself how many people in the midstream of life get the opportunity to consciously decide what they value, and based on those values how they will proceed with their life? It is truly an opportunity for a fresh start – an exciting life hack that ultimately produces a longed-for reboot. One way to coax the real self out of hiding is to connect with its deepest values.

## VALUES

What exactly are values you ask? Values are an individual's guiding principles or standards of behavior – an assessment of what is important in life – to you. Values are standards or ideals with which we guide our intentions, choices, decisions and behaviors. Truth, justice, kindness, love, integrity, family, belonging, for example are values that most people aspire to use to guide their lives. More specific values could be: meaningful work, education, personal growth, competency, nature, music, art, travel, financial security, safety, physical fitness, etc. Only you determine what matters to you and those values will, hopefully, determine how you spend your time and energy.

Once you have clarified what you value, you will better understand the direction you need to take and hopefully what is blocking you from proceeding in that direction. Frank Sonnenberg, in his book *"Follow Your Conscience: Make a Difference in Your Life & in the Lives of Others"*, says, *"Values are like a pilot's flight plan ... without them you're flying blind."* Here are more questions you can use to help you delve into the needs and longings of your true self so that you are not flying blind:

## MORE QUESTIONS TO CLARIFY CURRENT VALUES:

169.  What subjects or topics always seem to grab your attention?

170.  What activities are you drawn to, even if you have had minimal experience with them?

171.  Are there individuals you admire? Name a few.

172.  What do those individuals believe, stand for, or do, that you admire?

173.  If there were no obstacles, how would you want to spend your time and energy?

174.  Analyze the answers to the above 5 questions for clues to things (values) your real self prefers?

175.  How often do you find yourself holding back from expressing what matters to you?

176.  What exactly is the fear blocking you from expressing your deepest values?

177.  Is that fear really still relevant now that you are out of the cult or free from the abuse?

178.  What are your governing values now that you are free of the abusive system's values?

179.  Do you know the difference between an espoused value and a value lived via actions? Describe any values you espouse but do not actually live. Why is that?

180.  Are you aware that the values you live (by your actions) are your true values?

181.  Have you ever done a "values clarification" exercise? Such an exercise helps you find which values resonate with you and then determine if you are actually manifesting those values in your life. Knowing your true values will help you make better choices

and decisions, set more relevant goals, and better chart the path to reach them.

182. What, for example, were you required to value in your family or in the cult that may not be what your newly-emerging true self values?

183. Can you look for clues to what your authentic self values by reflecting on the books you like to read, the movies you prefer, the magazines you purchase, the websites you follow, the places you go, what the people you may secretly envy do in their life?

184. How can you bring more creative passion, more of what you value into your life?

Values change over a lifetime. We can feel stuck or unable to move forward because we are trying to live life from values imposed upon us or values we took on as teenagers. When you leave a belief system, you have to take time to evaluate which beliefs and values you want to keep and which to release. It is also important to determine if the values we espouse (say matter to us) are truly the values we live. Time to refresh your values.

**A VALUES CLARIFICATION EXERCISE** will help you identify values you had to set aside to survive. You can clarify your values using the values list provided on the next two pages.

Using pencil, highlight values on the 250+ list that currently resonate with you. There are no right or wrong answers. Values are unique to each individual. There may be many that feel important, but are not necessarily the ones you want to underpin your life right now. There will be others you can easily dismiss as totally unimportant for you at this point in your life.

Mark only the values that hold a high level of importance for you now. Once you have selected the most important values, go on to **select seven** of those that are the most significant. Some values may carry an equal weight – just select your top seven values ... as best you can. Then do the Guided-Imagery Values Experience that follows.

## VALUES CLARIFICATION 'MENU' - 1

| | | |
|---|---|---|
| acceptance | contentment | family |
| accomplishment | continuous Improvement | fearlessness |
| accountability | contribution | feelings |
| accuracy | control | fidelity |
| achievement | conviction | fitness |
| adaptability | cooperation | flexibility |
| adventure | courage | focus |
| altruism | courtesy | foresight |
| ambition | creativity | fortitude |
| amusement | curiosity | freedom |
| assertiveness | | friendship |
| agency | decisiveness | fun |
| authenticity | dedication | |
| authority | dependability | generosity |
| autonomy | determination | genius |
| awareness | democracy | giving |
| | development | goodness |
| balance | devotion | grace |
| beauty | dignity | gratitude |
| belonging | discipline | growth |
| boldness | discovery | |
| bravery | diversity | happiness |
| | drive | hard work |
| calm | | harmony |
| candor | effectiveness | health |
| caring | efficiency | honesty |
| certainty | empathy | honor |
| challenge | empowerment | hope |
| change | endurance | humility |
| charity | energy | humor |
| citizenship | engagement | |
| cleanliness | enjoyment | imagination |
| clarity | enthusiasm | impact |
| collaboration | environment | improvement |
| comfort | equality | inclusiveness |
| commitment | ethics | independence |
| common sense | excellence (personal) | individuality |
| communication | excitement | innovation |
| community | expertise | inspiration |
| compassion | exploration | integrity |
| competence | expressiveness | intelligence |
| confidence | | influence |
| connection | fairness | ingenuity |
| consciousness | faith | innovation |
| consistency | fame | intellectualism |

## VALUES CLARIFICATION 'MENU' - 2

joy
justice

kindness
knowledge

law
leadership
learning
leisure
liberty
logic
love
loyalty

mastery
maturity
meaning
meaningful work
mindfulness
moderation
motivation

nature

openness
optimism
order
organization
originality
open-mindedness

passion
patience
peace
performance
persistence
playfulness
pleasure
poise
potential
power
presence
prestige
privacy
productivity

professionalism
prosperity
purpose

quality

realistic
reciprocity
recognition
recreation
reflection
relationships
respect
responsibility
restraint
results
reverence
rigor
risk
romance

safety
satisfaction
security
self-awareness
self-care
self-control
self-development
self-expression
self-realization
self-reliance
selflessness
self-respect
self-supporting
sensitivity
sensuality
serenity
service
sexuality
sharing
significance
silence
simplicity
supportiveness
skillfulness
smart

solitude
spirituality
spontaneity
stability
status
stewardship
strength
structure
success
support
sustainability (environment)
success

talent
teamwork
temperance
thoughtfulness
tolerant
tough
traditional
tranquility
transparency
trust
truth

valor,
variety
victory
vigor
vision
vitality

wealth
wisdom
wonder

ADD OTHER VALUES HERE:

## A GUIDED-IMAGERY VALUES EXPERIENCE

*Imagine that you are on an important trek up a sacred mountain. You have been told that at the summit of this mountain you will understand your life, your purpose, and your path forward more clearly than you ever have before. You prepare a backpack with essentials for such a day trip and you put your top **seven top values** (from the values clarification exercise) **in the backpack**. You must bring them with you on the trek up the mountain.*

*It is a beautiful day and as you walk the views take your breath away. There are four rest stations on the path up the mountain where you will encounter park custodians who are tasked to make sure you are okay and have the resources and directions you require.*

*As you walk upward you see the first rest station in the distance and spot the park custodian waiting for you. After a brief chat, the custodian encourages you to continue your climb and wishes you well on the next phase of your journey. But first ... before you can proceed he tells you that you have to leave **two** of your seven values with him. Keep the values that are most important to you and hand over two values you are willing to release at this point.*

*This will not be easy, so take some time to think about which two values you are willing to leave behind ...........................................................*
*........................................... Once you have selected the two, hand them over to the custodian and continue your journey up the mountain trail.*

*You continue your climb happy that such a clear path has been made for you. It is the time of year you most enjoy and all the sights, smells and sounds remind you what a privilege it is to enjoy life on this planet. After a rigorous climb, you spot the second rest stop ahead and wave at the next custodian waiting for you there. You make use of resources available and prepare to set off again.*

*But first ... this custodian informs you that you again must leave **two** of the values in your backpack with her. Although this is difficult, you select two more values to leave behind. You are not allowed to say you would rather stop your climb than forfeit two more values. You have to give up another two values and continue on your trek. Choose two now ................................................................... Once you have* *selected two values, hand them to the custodian. You have three left in your backpack.*

*You continue your hike and the terrain is becoming steeper but the glorious weather and views distract you from the effort required. You are happy to see the next rest station and its custodian waiting for you with necessary resources. Yes, you guessed it … but this time you only have to leave* **one** *value behind. Choose which one …………………………………………………………………………… You now have two values left in your backpack.*

*You are now on the final stage of the trek, on the verge of reaching the pinnacle of the mountain where you will enjoy an amazing new perspective on your life. As you reach the peak of the mountain with your top two values in your backpack, you see there is a final resource station there and another custodian waiting to greet you. Once more you are told that to stand on the summit of the mountain you will have to surrender* **one** *of your two remaining values. Which one do you give up and which one do you keep? ………………………………………………………………… ……………………… Not an easy choice, but one you must make. Proceed to the peak with the last value in your backpack.*

*Now you stand on the summit – that is your life – with the* **one** *value you would not forfeit. Take time to absorb exactly what this value means to you and how, with this value and this higher perspective, you will use it to help yourself and the world.*

*After you have had time alone contemplating this new expansive perspective on your life, your treasured value, and your purpose, the custodian at this last resource station comes over and the two of you discuss how challenging it was to be asked to give up values and what you learned in the process.*

*The custodian tells you to treasure the learnings acquired and that on your journey back down to everyday life, you can pick up the values you had to leave behind with the other mountain custodians. You will surely use these other six values to underpin your new vision for your life.*

*Write about this guided imagery experience in your reboot journal.*

## MORE QUESTIONS ABOUT YOUR VALUES:

185. Why do you think the last value stayed with you until the end of the exercise?

186. What surprised you most about your reactions to giving up values?

187. Are your most highly-ranked, core values being expressed in your life now?

188. If *"no"*, why not?

189. What are your current passions?

190. What values lie at the core of your passion(s)?

191. When you think back on your biggest regrets in life, what values were not being expressed at the time?

192. What is blocking you now from enjoying the expression of other important core values?

193. What can you do to give a dormant value a venue for expression?

194. What values do you want to pass on to loved ones?

195. Write down your philosophy for living.

196. What values are implicit in, or support, that philosophy for living?

197. Has zeroing in on core values helped you better define your purpose? How?

198.  What could you do in the next couple of weeks that would be a life-enhancing expression of at least some of your core values?

199.  If there is a value that seems like it is impossible for you to manifest, are there ways you could incorporate parts or bits of it in your life ... in unique or unanticipated ways?

200.  How will your life improve once you are unstuck? List the ways in your journal.

You may notice that while you selected values on the values clarification menu, you kept some of the values instilled in you by your parents and/or a coercive group – that they still hold significance for you. That is fine and to be expected.

But moving a step beyond, and identifying what is important to the self you had to bury to survive, can be an important breakthrough. There are many benefits to knowing precisely what matters to you and what needs to be cherished and expressed at this point in your life. For example by clarifying your values in this way you will:

- feel more comfortable in your skin – knowing who you are and what you stand for.

- have the confidence of being self-validating rather than externally validated.

- make better decisions, knowing what matters and what principles guide you.

- be able to measure your progress in life according to your own standards.

- attract others with similar values. Knowing your values will make it clear who you wish to associate with and who you don't.

- better understand why certain situations disappoint or please you.

- feel more comfortable about following passions and gut instincts when they align with your values.

- reconnect with your purpose and power.

- enjoy more meaningful feelings about your life when aligned with your core values.

- shift out of a default self-referential mode of looking at life, and see life from a more altruistic perspective (e.g. as with your highest values at the summit of the mountain).

- be giving yourself a new experience and preparing for future new experiences.

As you continue with this reboot self-restoration process, you will have to determine what other things besides values you need to restore. Other things to consider restoring are:

- Self-care to enhance well-being (physical, emotional)
- life-balance
- peace of mind
- joy
- connection to self (knowing values will help with this connection)
- sense of freedom
- social supports
- connection to nature
- trust in self
- trust in world
- rightful place as full participant in life
- self-esteem
- self-direction
- sense of competence
- internal locus of control
- assertiveness
- emotional intelligence

- meaningful work
- understanding of the givens/realities of life

You might like to write the above bullet points (and any others you may have thought of that are not on the list) in your reboot journal and work with each one, examining if it is something you need to restore and how you plan to do that. There are very likely things that you did not allow your traumatic past to squash for you, while there will be others you have to reanimate in order to reboot your life. This, of course, takes time. Just being aware of what needs to be restored will be a great help. Healing, growth, and reboots begin with simple awareness and a gentle, mindful approach to the process.

Mindfulness is one of the best practices to help restore your values. When you mindfully notice what attracts and absorbs your attention, you will discover your passions and preferences. Mindfulness then gives you the time and ability to respond from your own values rather than from outdated, externally-imposed conditioning.

## Quotations to Inspire You to Restore Values:

*"Being connected to your own values makes you less likely to get stuck in a way that you're unable to see the opportunities that are available."* - Kelly McGonigal, Ph.D.

*"You don't have to live a lie. Living a lie will mess you up … It will warp your values."* - Gilbert Baker

*"Your personal core values define who you are."* - Tony Hsieh

*"A highly developed values system is like a compass. It serves as a guide to point you in the right direction when you are lost."* - Idowu Koyenikan

# 7. RE-EDUCATE & REWIRE

Re-educate definition: *"to train again; to rehabilitate through education."*
Rewire definition: *""…. to make lasting and usually beneficial changes to the neurological or psychological functioning of a person or brain…"* Merriam-Webster

I F YOU WERE in a cult you know that access to information was strictly controlled. You were manipulated to feel afraid of information sourced anywhere but in the group. You were told *"worldly"* information could be *"demon-inspired"* and that it would lead you away from *"the truth"*. Even if you had a longing to learn more, you would set aside the impulse and busy yourself with, for example, *"theocratic activities"* and *"theocratically-sourced (god-sourced) information"*.

Now out of the abusive system you are finally free to indulge your curiosity. You can be current with developments in science, culture, the arts, history, country, neighborhood, etc. Humans are wired to be curious, ask questions, find solutions, adjust, change, and begin again. You do not want to remain caught in the limited, repressive operating system while trying to create a new life.

Part of the old operating system that developed so I could survive in a stifling cult milieu, was to feign illness. It was the only way to slip past the oppression of JW controls, demands and expectations. Being 'under the weather' allowed one to miss a meeting, get out of going from door-to-door, or generally just be exempt from all the unreasonable expectations.

So I feigned illness as frequently as I thought I could get away with - without my mother suspecting. Since I did not want to outright lie, I scanned my body to find an ache or ailment that could necessitate staying home to rest and recover, and I was usually able to find something to serve the purpose. Supposed illness afforded me time to relax, sleep, study, read, watch TV, or commiserate with friends from school.

The unfortunate thing is once out of the cult, the pattern of ailments appearing when there was anything I wanted to avoid, continued. If my nervous system detected any sign of resistance about doing something JW-related it would try to accommodate that resistance by producing a physical ailment. This old, desperate maneuver to have a bit of privacy and personal time while a teenager became quite counterproductive when, as an adult, I found myself battling mysterious symptoms right before things I *really wanted* to do. Just the excitement of an anticipated activity could produce unwanted physical symptoms.

Consciously unaware of what was really going on, I had no choice but to become adept at dealing with these physical issues. I had to step up and face new experiences, obligations, challenges and exciting opportunities in spite of my trigger-happy nervous system that produced symptoms at the least sign of anticipation, anxiety, or excitement. I learned to live my life around this irksome pattern.

I had unwittingly set my mind/body into a default pattern that was so unnecessary, all due to a misguided coping strategy from my youth in a controlling cult. This defense strategy helped me then, but interfered with my life once I was out. It was a problem I needed to address by doing some serious research and ultimately re-educating and rewiring my nervous system.

The research revealed just what I suspected: I had inadvertently wired my brain and nervous system to produce physical symptoms upon any sign of psychological or emotional discomfort. It seemed this defense mechanism now had difficulty differentiating between anxiety and excitement – and the symptoms would arise even before activities I *really wanted* to engage in.

Research by Dr. Stephen Porges on the vagus nerve, an important part of the autonomic (parasympathetic) nervous system, helped me better understand these maladaptive patterns. I included some of that information – about how to rewire our brain away from the accommodations made by it to deal with undue controls and adversity – in my book "*Shunned: A Survival Guide*" and it is excerpted here in The Appendix.

If you are reading this book and have read any of my other books, you are already re-educating yourself in order to rewire your brain after adversity – to get unstuck, and to move ahead with your life – even if you are still unsure exactly where you are headed.

As you continue to re-educate yourself about recovery, the change process, and your brain's incredible ability to rewire itself after trauma, you will identify your particular habitual ways of coping with perceived threats to your identity and freedom.

## QUESTIONS ABOUT HOW YOU CAN RE-EDUCATE YOURSELF:

201.   Have you assessed and owned your existing base of knowledge?

202.   Where did you learn most of what you understand about life and the world around you?

203.   Have you discovered or tapped into what most deeply excites you? For example?

204.   How are you now using your existing base of knowledge and existing strengths to move forward?

205.   Have you identified any gifts that came as a result of your suffering? Describe them.

206.   What resources are available to you that you are not yet using? Describe.

207.   What existing knowledge, talents, skills, competencies need to find greater expression in your life? Describe.

208.   Have you applied your intent and your energy to use what you already know to propel you forward in your life? Explain?

209. With hindsight, can you see growth and strength you have not acknowledged? Such as?

210. How did the cult or parents trap you in an anti-education mindset and hinder your launch into life?

211. Do you see that despite any failure to launch, you are now responsible to take the steps necessary to build a rewarding life?

212. Can you re-awaken any curiosity crushed by membership in a controlling cult? How?

213. Have you mined any missteps or failures for growth and strength? What did you find?

214. Have you learned about Post-Trauma Growth? (See *"Shunned: A Survival Guide"*, Chapter 17)

215. Have you found access to the wisdom and knowing of your inner voice? Examples?

216. Can you see the opportunities and advantages that came along with the crisis of leaving the cult or abusive family situation and the challenging aftermath? Describe.

217. Have you considered that growth and progress rarely come on their own but rather require a crisis, an upset, a breaking apart, a blockage?

218. Have you recognized that you cannot create a new life for yourself without disrupting or overthrowing the old?

219. Can you now reframe leaving the abusive system from a crisis to an awakening, an education, and an opening?

220. What new information is now demanding your attention? Explore this in your journal.

221. How can you be more receptive to new information?

222. Are there knowledge gaps that need to be attended to? Describe.

223. How are you making up for lost time spent in a closed, controlling system?

224. Can you make yourself an expert (over time) in a subject area that excites you? How?

225. Can you become a self-directed, life-long learner? How?

226. Are there areas of learning you assume are not open to you? Which ones?

227. With all the new platforms for learning out there, is that still true?

228. Can you make it your goal to build a relevant skill set to offer today's marketplace?

229. Where would you go to learn these skills or can you learn them on your own?

230. Could you apprentice with someone or ask to shadow/train with someone already working in the field?

231. Could you make use of online learning platforms or take courses offered online by experts in the field(s) that interests you?

After doing research about a topic, take time away from the research or reading and allow your unconscious mind to sit with the information and produce relevant insights. You could pose a question to your unconscious, go about other activities, and wait for your unconscious to reveal the answer – with an idea, an "aha" moment, or a dream. The act of thinking about and answering the 350+ questions in this book will set your subconscious to work on developing new ideas for your life.

Your subconscious mind is designed to work on the input it is given and produce answers or intuitions. They will be *your* answers – based on your unconscious mind's knowledge of all you have been through and all you have learned.

This chapter is designed to help remind you that your recovery from an oppressive family situation and/or cult indoctrination and deception is not complete if you have not used your newfound freedom to re-educate yourself – be it formally or informally.

You are now free to be curious. Stay current. Read. Study. Take courses. By so doing you will greatly expand your perspective, options and universe. You will develop a better understanding of the world and your place in it.

Re-education will not just introduce you to new subject matter and skills. The very act of learning new things will help rewire your brain. Learn something new just for the sheer pleasure and enjoyment of it. What freedom! Have you taken advantage of this opportunity? It's time to turn your suffering and struggle into learning that shines a light on the next steps to your goals. Your efforts at re-education will help you get unstuck.

## NEW EXPERIENCES REWIRE THE BRAIN

The best education includes *experiential* components: learning by doing rather than learning only by listening, watching, studying or reading. By gifting yourself with new experiences, whether formal ones or not, you discover what interests and excites you. New experiences stimulate your brain and are especially important to help rewire a brain and nervous system that have been locked into a fight, flight or freeze response due to trauma.

New experiences are also one of the best ways to get unstuck and one of the best ways to re-educate and redefine yourself once out of an abusive situation. Psychotherapist, Bill O'Hanlon affirms this when he says: "*The brain tends to go in grooves unless you can jump into other grooves. And one of the ways to change the grooves is to stimulate the brain in a new way.*"

New, corrective experiences are also the best way to disrupt counterproductive patterns because they create new neuropathways in the brain. This is called **neuroplasticity**. Dr. Michael Merzenich, pioneer in the science of neuroplasticity defines it as follows: "*...the brain's ability to change its anatomical, neurochemical, and functional performance status across the lifespan.*" (Plasticity is defined as**:** pliability, flexibility, ability to adapt.) With a new experience old wiring is disrupted and weakened and new wiring is created.

Our brains are wired to be able to change. We can break bad habits. We can learn new languages. We can acquire new skills. We can adapt to changing circumstances. Our brains and our patterns of thinking, feeling, and living are not set in stone. However, to enjoy the benefits of new experiences, we have to move past any patterns of avoidance, apathy, helplessness, fear, and isolation we may have learned in a coercive control environment.

Endurance athlete and writer Christopher Bergland says, *"One could speculate that this process opens up the possibility to reinvent yourself and move away from the status quo or to overcome past traumatic events that evoke anxiety and stress. Hardwired fear-based memories often lead to avoidance behaviors that can hold you back from living your life to the fullest."*

We are each born with more neural synapses than we will ever use. It is okay to allow some to die off from lack of reinforcement and disuse. If you are not reinforcing old patterns of self-protection due to trauma, abuse, indoctrination and limitation, those debilitating neural pathways become disconnected from the brain's wiring. They weaken from disuse.

The science of neuroplasticity also tells us we do not have to wait for the neurons that cause or remind us of pain to die off from lack of use. We can actually take a conscious role in pruning them away. We do this by not giving the old patterns that hurt us or keep us stuck any reinforcement, support, interest, or attention – and by replacing them with *new experiences* that require new wiring and that then begin to dominate our consciousness.

Human brains thrive and grow on novelty, challenge and change. To reset or rewire your brain away from any hurt, fear, indoctrinated beliefs, old habits, and/or unskillful patterns you need to be pro-active in kicking your brain out of its comfort zone and into the rewiring zone by engaging in experiences that are unfamiliar, challenging, and even mentally taxing.

Clinician Ian Cleary says, *"Any brain changes are at the expense of other changes. The development of these parts of our brain that effort-lessly trigger anxiety, is at the detriment of the ones that aid calmness & confidence ... it is not enough to just stop anxiety in any given moment, which is often people's focus. The anxiety wiring is still there and wait-ing to be triggered.* **We need to create competitive wiring.** *We need to* *create specific wiring of what we want to achieve which is 'competitive wiring' to the problem. Without this we loop endlessly in anxiety with no new neural pathway to take us forward."* (Bold added.)

Reread Ian Cleary's words just above. We need to create *"competitive wiring"* to the detriment of old wiring. How do we create competitive wiring? By giving ourselves new and challenging experiences.

If you've never played chess – take up the challenge. If you've never done a New York Times crossword or Sudoku puzzle – take up the challenge. Activities that are novel or challenging rewire your brain away from being stuck. New experiences are the best reboot! And ... after being repressed and stuck in a repressive family or cult we surely crave new experiences!

We wire our brains negatively when we engage in negative self-talk, persist with undesirable habits, indulge in destructive addictions, reinforce perceived limitations, etc. The more we repeat behaviors, the more brain neurons are relegated to that particular neural pathway. The phrase coined by Canadian neuropsychologist, Donald Hebb, way back in 1949: *"Neurons that fire together, wire together"* applies here. If we keep firing the thinking, behaviors and habits that keep us stuck or keep us feeling helpless or hopeless, we reinforce (*wire together*) those neural pathways and further imbed the pattern. We remain stuck. We actually deepen the very rut we want to climb out of.

To change the pattern and get unstuck we have to disrupt the pattern and provide the brain with new information it has to record, organize, and link up to other neural pathways. It takes work and we have to be willing to experience the temporary malaise of moving away from our habitual comfort zone. Thought patterns, trigger memories, activated nervous system alarms do not change on their own, but they do with determination and persistent effort. With fresh experiences old debilitating patterns can die off and room is made for the new.

No, new experiences will not alter a painful past, but they will help change our relationship to what happened in the past – and even more importantly to what is happening in the present. New experiences will push past disappointments and regrets to the back of your mind. You will be rewiring your brain away from the old voices telling you what you cannot do, away from a shame-based self, away from indoctrinated fears, away from perceptions of helplessness. Well-selected experiences wire your brain toward competence, responsiveness, positivity, and resilience.

You have it in your power to rewire or reset your brain away from lingering family controls and/or cult-sourced helplessness. Giving yourself the gift of new experiences is called *self-directed brain plasticity*. It could also be called a brain reboot! Forcing your brain to encode new experiences is like keeping your brain's software updated. Making new healthy lifestyle choices is one way to support your brain's hardware. Physical exercise, healthy sleep patterns, optimal nutrition, and even intermittent fasting are all thought to enhance or boost neuroplasticity.

Mental health writer Debbie Hampton on her website *"The Best Brain Possible"* gives several suggestions on how to *"drive neuroplastic change externally"*. She suggests that we: *"... try something new, mix things up, turn off the GPS, exercise in a new way, train your brain, take a trip, be social."*

Why not try new experiences as simple, reasonable, easy and inexpensive as:

- listening to a new type of music
- reading a new genre of book
- learning a new musical instrument
- cooking and eating a new type of cuisine
- enriching your home environment – (enriched environments benefit adults as well as children)
- trying a different form of physical exercise
- allowing yourself to get lost on a walk and using your instincts to get your bearings
- taking a different route while walking your dog
- exploring a different part of your city

- using your non-dominant hand to write, draw or text
- taking a time-out to detox from social media, digital devices, TV
- striking up a conversation with a stranger
- seeking out friends outside of your normal social milieu
- learning a new language
- taking a course
- learning to juggle
- taking up yoga
- doing a Sudoku each day
- getting and training a pup
- rearranging your desk so you have to use your brain to find things
- changing up your morning schedule, etc., etc.

You can also rewire your brain from the inside by using mindfulness, meditation, and visualization (visualization is a form of virtual practice which engages and stimulates the brain). Norman Doidge, M.D. says, *"Brain scans also show that those who do "mental practice" develop changes in the same brain areas, to roughly the same extent, as those who do "physical practice"*. John B. Arden, Ph.D. adds, *"Not only does behavior change the structure of the brain through neuroplasticity; just thinking about or imagining particular behaviors can change brain structure as well."*

If you wait until you feel like initiating a new experience it will probably never happen. The moment you notice the impulse to initiate a new experience you have to act immediately. Author and founder of *The Game Changers Academy*, Peter Voogd tells us we have to plan and act first, and pay attention to any feelings about it *after* we act. Since most of us are prone to prefer our comfort zone, our feelings will usually nudge us toward comfort and inertia rather than novelty.

In a similar vein, motivational speaker Mel Robbins created a *"5 Second Rule"* that says the moment you notice an impulse to take a life-enhancing decision or action, you have to do so right away: *"If you* have an impulse to act on a goal you must physically move within 5 seconds or your brain will kill the idea." The status quo will usually win out if we don't act right away, because we can talk ourselves out of almost anything that requires effort or involves the unknown.

Push past this common human tendency and give yourself the gift of new experiences – even when you don't feel like it. You will be rewiring your brain to be more comfortable with change. If you want to reboot your life you have to be willing to try new things and take action on your own behalf. The good news is that the actions themselves can turn out to be quite enjoyable.

## Quotations About the Value of New Experiences and How They Rewire the Brain:

*"Neuroplasticity is the property of the brain that enables it to change its own structure and functioning in response to activity and mental experience."* - Norman Doidge, M.D.

*"... the very structure of our brain — the relative size of different regions, the strength of connections between one area and another — reflects the lives we have led. Like sand on a beach, the brain bears the footprints of the decisions we have made - the skills we have learned, the actions we have taken."* - Sharon Begley

*"Your brain is a relentless shape-shifter, constantly rewriting its own circuitry — and because your experiences are unique, so are the vast detailed patterns in your neural networks. Because they continue to change your whole life, your identity is a moving target; it never reaches an end point."* - David Eagleman, neuroscientist

*"The idea that the brain can change its own structure and function through thought and activity is, I believe, the most important alteration in our view of the brain since we first sketched out its basic anatomy and the workings of its basic component, the neuron."* - Norman Doidge, M.D.

*"Nothing speeds brain atrophy more than being immobilized in the same environment: the monotony undermines our dopamine and attentional systems crucial to our brain plasticity."* - Norman Doidge

*"Where attention goes, neural firing flows, and neural connection grows."* - Daniel J. Siegel

*"Clearly, the brain can exert a powerful grip on one's life — but only if you let it. The good news is that you can overcome the brain's control and rewire your brain to work for you by choosing to act in healthy, adaptive ways."* - Jeffrey M. Schwartz, M.D.

There is no better way to reboot your life and get unstuck than to reassess and challenge the way you think and act. The simple act of choosing new experiences for yourself each day can rewire your brain away from limitation, stagnation, helplessness, inability to make choices, and reluctance to take actions.

Perhaps you did not realize that while you were doing the Values Clarification Exercise in the last chapter, you were probably engaged in a new experience that helps reset your brain away from being stuck in old patterns. Allow me to share a new experience that I orchestrated, strongly resisted, and eventually pushed through, that helped move me out of limiting, cult-sourced value judgments and comfort-seeking patterns.

## A PERSONAL EXAMPLE OF RELUCTANT "REWIRING"

While attending university I enrolled in an elective course called "*Drama Therapy*", in the Department of Creative Arts Therapies, wanting to expand my skills as a therapist. It was a yearlong course where students learned the power of embodying and dramatizing psychological issues. This was an experiential course and students would learn by physically performing their own issues under the supervision of therapists/professors. The learnings from these dramatizations were then deepened via analysis with the therapists/professors, and with written papers summarizing the knowledge and skills we were working to master.

*"Drama Therapy is the intentional use of drama and/or theater processes to achieve therapeutic goals. Drama therapy is active and experiential. This approach can provide the context for participants to tell their stories, set goals and solve problems, express feelings, or achieve catharsis."* - North American Drama Therapy Association

Walking in the classroom on the first day I saw all the desks were moved to the back of the room and everyone was seated in a circle on the floor – all the cool, young students – who I quickly imagined to be much less inhibited than this cult-raised, almost forty, suburban mother.

I felt I had made a mistake by registering for the course. Being from a different background and generation than the rest of the students, I doubted that I would be able to be as free, open and expressive. I was too self-conscious to walk out and willed myself to join the circle on the floor.

This course was not a required one in order to graduate and it could easily be dropped in order to spare myself the embarrassment of having to participate in dramatic scenes acting out psychological issues in front of people so much younger than myself. Trying to talk myself out of continuing, I mentally made a quick list of many good reasons to drop out, but somehow in spite of the misgivings I stayed. The students turned out to be open, friendly and inclusive, and I eventually forgot about the age difference and drastically different life experiences.

The first dramatized scene in which I was assigned to participate was with a handsome young man called 'Jagger'. ("Jagger" is a
pseudonym, but his real name was equally as 'edgy'.)

He looked even more intimidating than his name. He had spiked
'Mohawk-styled' bleached platinum hair, holes pierced in his earlobes
the size of a dime, tattoos on his arms and neck, spiked metal jewelry,
skinny knees taunting me from ripped jeans, and menacing, unlaced,
scuffed-up combat boots. Jagger and I worked well together and over
the year he often sought me out when the class was asked to divide
up and work in pairs.

One class assignment required each student to cast, script, and
re-enact a situation from their past where they had not been able to
say something they needed to say. The scenario I chose was when
my father returned to the family after having totally abandoned it for a
couple of years. My mother accepted him back on the condition that
he study cult publications every week with a JW elder and attend all
JW meetings.

I chose one student for the role of the psychotherapist attending
the drama therapy scene who would help us interpret and understand
the dynamics that played out in the scene, and cast two others in the
roles of my father and mother. Jagger was cast as the Jehovah's Witness elder.

The entire class giggled as Jagger sauntered into the scene carrying a dilapidated briefcase like an up-tight minister/elder would have
done. No one could have looked less like an elder, but Jagger played
the role well and once we all stopped giggling I was able to say what
I wished I could have said to that JW elder and my mother way back
then (e.g. *"how dare they put my father in a position where he would be
infantilized and shamed."*).

To my father I was finally able to say I realized what a double-bind
he was in, how much I regretted that he had to sit there and be humiliated by this self-aggrandizing elder. I was also able to communicate
that I now realized this weekly study requirement imposed by my misguided, devout mother may have been a part of his decision to

permanently abandon the family - and the seemingly non-negotiable requirement to be one of Jehovah's Witnesses.

Image depicting a random Drama Therapy class.

This elective Drama Therapy course taught me much. Each class turned out to be a new experience that forced me out of my rigid, old, cultish comfort zone. With each drama assignment I thought "*Oh no – what will I have to do now*?" As a recent ex-JW I still preferred to exclude myself and not reveal much about myself to anyone.

Each assignment required that I expose more than I anticipated and dig deeper into my well of pain than I wanted to in front of a university class. However, each of those new experiences turned out to be an opportunity to learn something new about expressive therapies that I could eventually incorporate into my work as a psychotherapist. It was also a pivotal part of rewiring my cult-indoctrinated brain away from limiting values, judgments, expectations, and assumptions.

Jagger – whose appearance frightened and intimidated me at first – turned out to be brilliant, insightful and caring. Now *that* created many new neural connections in my judgmental, cult-educated brain! He often cast me in scenes to represent his psychoanalyst mother and I cast him in scenes to play my absent, cult-averse father. He played the role of my father with sensitivity.

I would have missed so much, on so many levels, if I had denied myself those challenging new experiences because of my initial resistance. Trust me, the incredible value of rewiring your brain by simply gifting yourself with new experiences may be one of the most important things you learn from this book! Try to push past any resistance you have to new experiences if you want to reboot your life.

## Quotations to Inspire You About the Need to Re-Educate & Rewire:

*"The best thing for being sad ... is to learn something. "* - T. H. White

*"Unless new experiences cause a rewiring of the old circuits, the patterns of coping we learn as toddlers become our default responses to life's perils and pitfalls."* - Linda Graham, MFT

*"You raise your standards every time when you – ignore the lizard brain, say no to distractions, delay gratification or choose voluntary discomfort."* - Prakhar Verma

*"Resilient people turn frustrating situations into opportunities to learn something new. Although they don't want bad things to happen, they adapt to bad circumstances by focusing on hidden opportunities."* - John B. Arden, Ph.D.

*"All life is an experiment. The more experiments you make the better."* - Ralph Waldo Emerson

# 8. RESPOND

Respond definition: ""... *to react in response.*" Responsible/Responsibility definition: *"moral, legal, or mental accountability; able to answer for one's conduct and obligations; able to choose for oneself between right and wrong.*" Merriam-Webster

A
S SAID IN a previous chapter, while writing my first two books I realized I still had unresolved issues dating back to the controls and stifling environment of the cult in which I was raised and needed to research psychosomatic issues and learn how to deal with them. I wanted to take *respon*sibility for how those issues were still affecting me. They were sourced in attempts to cope with cult controls, but I was still dealing with some in spite of having left and constructed a good new life.

To continue to endlessly blame my issues on the cult would be counterproductive. The cult would never step up to help resolve them. I had to take responsibility for what was happening with my body/mind/life. I had to assume the work of getting unstuck. While there may be initial resistance to taking responsibility for things we did not cause, what choice do we have if we want to move forward? Notice any resistance to taking responsibility and find your way to do it anyway. The first act of a successful reboot is assuming responsibility for initiating one.

You will find just the act of taking responsibility will empower you and provide some relief. Once you assume responsibility you will stop waiting for a miracle to help you move forward and will get to work on what you can do to take control of, and improve, your life. With this book you are being encouraged to take responsibility to:

- *review and reassess* the effects trauma had upon you and your life (Chapter 2)

- *record and document* the story/narrative you tell about your life (Chapter 3)

- *release* unnecessary, trauma-sourced burdens you have been carrying (Chapter 4)

- *recognize and reassess* maladaptive mind-sets and personas you employ (Chapter 5)

- *restore* your connection to your authentic self and its core values (Chapter 6)

- *re-educate and rewire* your brain away from trauma with new experiences (Chapter 7)

- *respond* by being willing to step up to do the hard work of change (Chapter 8)

- *re-imagine* possibilities and take concrete steps to produce them (Chapter 9)

- *recalibrate* internal psychological dynamics (Chapter 10)

- *revisit and refresh* your relationship to pain, guilt, time and self-care (Chapter 11)

- *reconnect* with "the world" by building a new circle of relationships (Chapter 12)

- *reboot* your life while learning to *relax* and *receive* new insights (Chapter 12)

The life hacks provided throughout this book will help you find ways to step up to create the personalized new experiences that will re-wire *your* brain and reboot *your* life.

The adverse event of being raised in an abusive family, raised in a cult (or converted to join one), spending years living under harsh controls, leaving the oppressive situation, and suffering all the repercussions for so doing, can have an incredible impact on our life. Coercive controls are so powerful that they can shape our life to the extent we may think the trauma or abuse has determined our fate. However, this is not true. There are millions of people who have left coercive control situations and moved on to create fulfilling lives for themselves. With a little time, reflection, assumption of responsibility, reboot work, and gifting yourself with new challenges, you will too!

## QUESTIONS TO HELP ACCEPT RESPONSIBILITY:

232. Have you perhaps resigned yourself to accepting the events of your past as your fate?

233. How is that working for you?

234. Describe examples of people you know of who took responsibility to make sure their fate was not determined by their past.

235. How do you avoid taking responsibility for your current situation?

236. How long are you willing to suffer the effects of avoiding personal responsibility for your unsatisfactory, stuck life situation?

237. How might *you* be getting in your own way?

238. Are you taking responsibility to tell the truth to yourself?

239. If you are in therapy, are you telling the whole story and the whole truth to the therapist?

240. Do you realize if you keep important events, double-binds, feelings, etc. hidden from the therapist, you are hindering their ability to help you?

241. Are you ready to own that staying stuck could be an inside job that can only be changed by the work you do?

If you are reading this book, we can safely assume you are ready to challenge assumptions about trauma, from whatever source, forever defining your fate. Although you probably bear little to no responsibility for being abused, indoctrinated, controlled, exploited and/or shunned, you do bear responsibility for the attitude you take toward that unfortunate past and what you do to respond to it now.

In the cult or a controlling family we were groomed *not* to take responsibility for our lives. It was made clear early on that our parents, the Bible, the cult leaders, and/or their literature would tell us exactly how to live our lives and inform us how to respond to any circumstances that arose. We had many restrictions imposed upon us and were made to feel disloyal if we dared to have responses of our own. We were told how our future would unfold and that to live to enjoy the promised rewards all that was required was our unquestioning obedience.

In such a stultifying environment one is groomed to wait to be told what to do – to not respond. We handed over the responsibility for our future to others. We were discouraged from acting on our own behalf. In fact, we learned that rewards and punishments were out of our control. The leaders or our parents cultivated degrees of "learned helplessness" in their members – all the better to control them and have them do all the grunt work for their goals. As well as having to deal with learned helplessness, we may now also have to deal with being responsibility-impaired. Fortunately, with a little effort, those two 'conditions' can be reversed.

In a cult-like environment there is no option or support to develop competence in anything that does not favor the group's goals. Subject to those controls we stop dreaming or planning for our future. Our ability to respond to life's ups and downs is thereby diminished because the manipulators manage every aspect of our life.

Thus we develop what is called an *external* locus of control (*"How do they want me to respond?"*) instead of an *internal* locus of control (*"How do I want to respond?"*). Unfortunately, we can drag this mindset with us into our new free life.

Another effect of having been a member of a controlling cult, group or family – especially if we spent our childhood in one – is that the abuse, trauma and pain of being manipulated and repressed means we are often predisposed to seek emotional, psychological and physical safety rather than new challenges and growth. A need to feel safe seems to trump all other needs.

## QUESTIONS ABOUT THE HABIT OF ALWAYS SEEKING TO FEEL SAFE:

242.  How is your current life designed around seeking safety rather than seeking new experiences, looking for opportunities, taking risks?

243.  How might you be stuck in an old, 'safe', comfort zone that no longer serves you and keeps you stuck?

244.  Are you aware the price you pay for not fulfilling your potential (e.g. staying 'safe' – even from difficult feelings) is guilt, self-alienation, and even self-contempt?

245.  Have you considered that feeling stuck in an unlived life can result as much from what you omit taking responsibility for and omit doing, as from what you actually do?

246.  What have you been omitting doing that needs to be done to move forward?

247.  What has been the cost of such omissions and avoidance?

248.  How long are you willing to pay that price?

249.  When you look back at this stuck period, what will you wish you had done differently?

250.  Stuck in a pattern of avoidance of responsibility or avoidance of emotional pain, what opportunities or options might you not be seeing now?

251.  For example, do you allow yourself to slow down, pause and allow good feelings, successes, important insights, peek experiences to sink into your consciousness?

Fritz Perls, who originated a form of therapy called "Gestalt", which among other things accentuates the importance of personal responsibility, tells us: *"As long as you fight a symptom, it will become worse. If you take responsibility for what you are doing to yourself, how you produce your symptoms, how you produce your illness, how you produce your existence – the very moment you get in touch with yourself – growth begins, integration begins."*

Perls went a step further and helped his clients recognize that helplessness is often unwillingness. This is an important insight for anyone who feels stalled after recovering from trauma. Your feeling of helplessness may actually be unwillingness. Are you willing to do what is necessary to reboot your life?

## QUESTIONS ABOUT HELPLESSNESS:

252.  How might any helplessness you feel actually be unwillingness to take responsibility for making your life better?

253.  How can you begin to confront, wrestle with, and respond to a counterproductive, erroneous perception of being helpless or unable?

254.  Again, what price are you paying for the illusion of safety that your unwillingness to step out of your comfort zone seems to provide?

255.  How does unwillingness, avoidance, or seeming paralysis make you feel about yourself? Is it worth it?

256.  Are you willing to step up and take responsibility to make your life better?

Gary John Bishop tells us the first question he uses to respond to life's challenges is: *"Am I willing? … It [that question] pulls for a response … Its power is irresistible; I cannot escape its press for truth."* Are you willing?

Therapists are well aware when a client frequently responds to questions or suggestions by saying *"I don't know"*, *"Perhaps"*, *"Maybe"*, *"I'll try"*, *"I can't"*, *"I wouldn't be comfortable with that"*, or *"I don't know how"*, etc. they are fundamentally unwilling and, thereby, avoiding taking responsibility to do what is required.

When freshly out of a control milieu, a person may be looking for someone who will still assume the role of savior, caretaker, parent, protector, or decision-maker for them. So doing may help the person avoid the anxiety that comes with taking responsibility and embracing new challenges. Unfortunately, it also keeps them stuck and can ultimately drive them even further into feelings of apathy, passivity, anxiety, and/or depression.

If you want to change your life for the better, if you want to reboot your life, you must first look inside and ask yourself if you are willing to:

- tell the truth
- experience some discomfort in service of growth
- look deeply inside
- take responsibility
- reach out for help when needed
- step up and respond

If you are not willing, you are wasting your time. If you are not *really* willing, you will find a way to sabotage even your own attempts to change and move forward. No one else can reboot your life but you. But first you must be willing.

Conversely, it may be you need to itemize all the things you are now absolutely *unwilling* to endure – e.g. humiliation, shame, loneliness, stress, anxiety, half a life. Once you identify what you are unwilling to tolerate, you can then decide how you *will* respond in order to make the necessary changes. There are times when negative motivation can be powerful.

257. What 'comforts' have you finally had enough of and are willing to let go of?

258. What challenges are you now willing to take on?

If you have read my other books you may recall my comparing a cult to an ultimate *"eternal caretaker"* or a *"parental substitute"* who promises to take care of you in return for your obedience to their vision and rules. Irvin D. Yalom, in his book Existential Psychotherapy, warns us about succumbing to this kind of seduction: *"Others submerge their wishes in the infantile hope that eternal caretakers will be able to read their wishes for them. There is something infinitely reassuring about having someone else meet one's unexpressed wishes. Still others so fear abandonment by caretakers that they repress all direct expression of personal desire. They do not permit themselves the right to wish, as though their wishing would irritate, threaten, or drive away others."*

Do you relate to Yalom's description? Have you, based on past conditioning, even abdicated your right to wish? That is a signal you need to assume responsibility to take back your right to dream, to envision, to aspire, to wish, and to plan and determine your own future.

## MORE QUESTIONS RELATED TO TAKING PERSONAL RESPONSIBILITY:

259.  How might you be actively contributing to your 'stuck' situation?

260.  What choices are creating your life now?

261.  What avoidances are shaping your life?

262.  What are you refusing to do and then blaming the effects of the refusal on something outside of yourself?

263.  How are you unconsciously sabotaging your desire to and efforts to move forward?

264. Are you always waiting for things to happen? Why?

265. Do you know what you need to do, but do not want to do it?

266. Are you aiming too low?

267. Do you need to raise expectations of what you are capable of?

268. Do you realize that only you can do this for yourself?

269. Are you generally passive instead of pro-active?

270. Do you need to activate your will – your ability to act on your own behalf?

271. Do you need to come to terms with the reality that we are each responsible for creating the best life possible in accord with our circumstances?

272. Every life has undesirable, unalterable elements. Can you reframe that which you cannot change? Give examples.

273. Have you outgrown your present way of doing things and need to take responsibility for creating a new vision for your life?

274. How might you be re-victimizing yourself by remaining a casualty of the abuse (in your mind)?

275. Are there secondary gains (benefits) for remaining in the victim role?

276. How are you avoiding making choices or decisions that would help you move forward?

277. Are you avoiding challenging old assumptions about how you should live your life?

278. Have you taken on too many mundane, unnecessary responsibilities that keep you from contemplating new ways of operating?

279. Are you stuck in relationships that sap you of energy due to an ongoing power-struggle? Which ones? How, exactly, are you stuck?

280. Are you allowing short-term anxieties to keep you from creating a fresh vision for yourself and setting long-term goals?

281. Are you stuck in a pattern of always being busy, always having obligations, always surrounding yourself with people and pastimes?

282. Can you learn to spend a bit more time alone – where your mind is not bombarded with stimuli and you can generate ideas about how to move ahead with your life?

283. Have you thought about how many inner resources you may be ignoring or not yet cultivating? (Inner resources such as feeling your own strength, resilience, gratitude, memories of tenderness and belonging, moments of experiencing your own goodness, moments of confidence and competence; moments of sensing your deep connection to nature/the universe, etc.)

284. When you experience any of the above sweet moments can you take time to pause and allow them to be felt throughout your entire body – give them space to grow inside and become a significant part of your felt body/mind experience?

285. Are you aware that by doing this work (and answer these questions) you are actually taking responsibility to rewire your brain away from the overwhelming effects of trauma?

286. How can you strengthen you own will (power)?

You must take responsibility to learn ways of coming back to yourself after so many years of setting your true self aside to accommodate the expectations of others – skillful ways such as embracing:

- solitude
- silence
- quiet contemplation
- connection with Nature
- purposeful connection with your real Self
- meditation
- gratitude

- appreciation for your strength, resilience and fundamental goodness
- mindful awareness of inner and outer environments
- calm observation of patterns, feelings and needs

Skillful practices such as those above will help you show up for your own life and your own experiences. They also give you the time to install the empowering feelings that accompany good experiences, in your brain. As you turn your focus to the good, the more difficult feelings tied to the past will recede. As you show up for, and spend time with, your good experiences they will increasingly become internalized and become more available to you as constant inner resources.

Perhaps you have been trying to get unstuck, to move ahead without access to vital inner resources. That's too hard! Change that now. We all know how easy it is to dwell on our own negativity such as our fears, mistakes, humiliations, regrets, and resentments. As those thoughts repeat and repeat we unwittingly imbed their neural wiring in our brain. They then become the place from which we live and the soil that determines what and how we grow.

If instead, you allow good experiences to permeate your body/mind you will be helping to imbed (wire) those positive, empowering, restorative, calm experiences in your brain. We need to spend as much inner time with our good experiences as we do with our fears, worries and ruminations. How many of us do that? Spending time with the positive feelings that result from a good experience allows those good feelings to be encoded in the brain *"as a lasting neural trait"*.

Psychologist Hanson suggests it takes 10 to 20 seconds of allowing the good feeling to permeate our mind and body for the new neural connections to be formed. Surely, we want at least as many positive neural pathways as we have negative. This is transformational information. Use it!

*"Whenever you remember a particular event, your brain releases chemicals similar to those released when you originally input impressions of the event...In order to balance the bad memories and heal the deep*

*limbic part of our brain, it is important to remember the times of our life that were charged with positive emotions."* - Daniel G. Amen, M.D.

## TAKE RESPONSIBILITY FOR TELLING
## THE TRUTH TO YOURSELF

One of the main things we have to do when stuck is to make sure we are being truthful with ourselves. We need to check if we have glossed over experiences and the feelings that accompany them in order to cope.

If you are feeling unable to move forward with your life it could be that you are still operating in denial about how deeply you were affected. For example, if you are keeping a secret (for whatever reason) about any kind of abuse suffered, you may want to look at how that secret is affecting your ability to move ahead with your life. It requires a lot of mental, emotional and physical constriction to keep secrets or hold back (suppress) memories, and when we constrict ourselves in one area we may be unconsciously constricting ourselves in others. Fortunately, you are in charge of your life and your secrets – what you reveal and when or if.

What I am suggesting is that you take the personal risk to reflect upon secrets or information you hold back (especially from yourself) and how your life is being affected by them. I am not asking you to publicize anything – only asking that you, yourself, take the risk to own the truth of what happened, how it affected you, and how, knowing what you know now will you move forward into your future?

As well, are you telling yourself the truth about long-standing presumptions, resentments, stories, and any negative judgments about people or possibilities? What if some things you accept as givens about your life and the world are not actually true? Is there a way to find out?

Teacher Byron Katie has developed a set of killer questions to help return to the truth of any matter. After selecting a thought that causes stress or seems to be interfering with living a full life, she encourages us to ask four simple questions:

1) *Is it true?*

2) *Can you absolutely know it's true?*

3) *How do you react ... what happens, when you believe that thought?*

4) *Who would you be without the thought?*

***) After answering the four questions, she has you *turnaround the stressful thought* stating its opposite (there are usually several opposites). For example:

* Stressful thought: *"It's too late for me."*

* Turnaround thought: *"It's not too late for me"*.

Byron Katie then has you look for ways that the turnaround statement could be true, even though your first reaction is that it is not.

It only takes a few minutes to complete her four questions and the turnaround and it is shocking to discover how much of what we tell ourselves is not totally true.

If you want to examine the absolute truth about your most distressing thoughts and free yourself from the burden of not speaking the truth to yourself, go to Katie's website and download the free worksheets to help you work on the ways your thoughts and assumptions may be unnecessarily torturing you and holding you back.

Byron Katie's questions and turnaround are a powerful life hack you need to keep at hand! Write her 5 step formula (4 questions and the turnaround) in your reboot journal. Katie's website is "thework.com"

## TAKE RESPONSIBILITY FOR YOUR DECISION-MAKING

Our ability to make decisions may have been damaged by familial or cult indoctrination and controls. We were not allowed many opportunities to make important life decisions – they were all made for us. But now, assuming responsibility for our situation requires that we exercise our will and make choices and decisions. Not always easy, at first.

Every decision involves some loss. When we decide in favor of one action, it means we have to exclude or give up others. In fact, the word "decide" comes from the same root as the words *"homicide"*, *"suicide"*, *"genocide"*, *"infanticide"*, *"matricide"* etc. – all related to killing something. We may find ourselves avoiding decision-making because we want to keep all our options alive or open. We do not want to kill off any possibilities. We may, thereby, keep all our possibilities open – but go nowhere because we are stuck until we decide and act.

Dr. Yalom tells us, *"Decisions are very expensive, they cost you everything else."* However, life, change, movement forward, and progress all demand that we choose, that we make decisions. The mature adult, Yalom says, must decide to embrace the harsh realities of life, such as:

- *"Recognizing that life is at times unfair and unjust.*
- *Recognizing that ultimately there is no escape from some of life's pain and from death.*
- *Recognizing that no matter how close I get to other people, I must still face life alone.*
- *Facing the basic issues of my life and death, and thus living my life more honestly and being less caught up in trivialities.*
- *Learning that I must take ultimate responsibility for the way I live my life …"*

Post trauma, have you assumed the responsibility to decide to come to terms with the realities of life as outlined by Dr. Irvin Yalom? To move ahead with your life you must take responsibility and make decisions. Avoiding either will keep you stalled.

## Quotations to Inspire You About the Need for Responsibility:

*"Most people do not really want freedom, because freedom involves responsibility, and most people are frightened of responsibility."*
- Sigmund Freud

*"... each man is questioned by life; and he can only answer to life by answering for his own life; to life he can only respond by being responsible."* - *Viktor Frankl*

*"Either you control your destiny, or your destiny will control you. Life won't stop for your pauses and procrastinations. It won't stop for your confusion or fear. It will continue right along without you. Whether you play an active part or not, the show will go on."* - Gary John Bishop

*"Wisdom tells me I am nothing.*
*Love tells me I am everything.*
*Between the two, my life flows."*

- Sri Nisargadatta

# 9. RE-IMAGINE

Re-imagine definition: *"to form a new conception of; to imagine again or anew."* Merriam Webster

WHEN YOU LEAVE a high-control environment that imposes rules for your life, you lose the blueprint for your future or your ability to create one. As you re-educate yourself and redefine your world and what you want to experience in it, a new vision for your life should unfold. But first you need to have a good grasp on what you need, what you want, what you desire – who you are apart from the faulty, imposed blueprint of the coercive environment. Paying attention to your longings and daydreams is one way to identify unmet needs and unfulfilled wants.

Have you spent time really considering what it is you value, love, want, need, long for? If not, dedicate some time to re-imagining a life that includes your deepest longings and see what clues emerge about how to reformat your life. Use your journal to record these re-imaginings.

There are probably many unmet needs from your past life that you are now more aware of. Yet because you were not allowed to have personal aspirations, or to imagine a future of your own making, you may still not know exactly what you want. It takes time and reflection to determine your true desires.

The old paradigm/environment failed you. So what do you need now in order to move fully ahead with your one and only life – the next chapter of your story? What do you need? What do you want? Charles Eisenstein helps identify core human needs saying:

*"A multiplicity of basic human needs go chronically, tragically unmet in modern society. These include:*

- *the need to express one's gifts and do meaningful work*

- *the need to love and be loved*

- *the need to be truly seen and heard, and to see and hear other people*

- *the need for connection to nature*

- *the need to play, explore, and have adventures*

- *the need for emotional intimacy*

- *the need to serve something larger than oneself, and*

- *the need sometimes to do absolutely nothing and just be.*

*An unmet need hurts, and fulfilling a need feels good ... Pain and pleasure are the doorways through which we discover what we really want and really need."*

The stuck story you have been telling about your life can pop up unexpectedly even once you believe you have set it aside. Keep checking to make sure you are not just moving the old, limited puzzle pieces around. Keep imagining and re-imagining what it would take to create the future you need and want.

Are you, as Eisenstein suggests, using pain and pleasures as guides to what is missing in your life – pointers to your unmet needs? Existential psychiatrist Yalom begins each therapy session with the simple question *"Tell me what ails?"* Four little words that help evoke the hurt and pain the client is carrying, also reveal to Yalom what the client most needs. Allow your hurt and your ailments to be pointers to what is missing in your life – to what you need. When we are aware of what is missing, we know in what area to begin our re-imaginings. What is missing in your life? What does your pain say about what you need?

Charles Eisenstein adds: *"Because our deeper unmet needs were mostly invisible to us, and because they have been unmet for so long, our physical and mental systems have adapted around them so that the pain becomes subconscious, diffuse, latent. That makes it hard sometimes to identify what the unmet need is."*

It is my hope that the many questions in this book will not only help you identify unmet needs but also help you find the way and the will to begin to fulfill them.

Engage in new experiences that provide pleasure and joy. Allow yourself to re-imagine the life you denied to yourself or that was denied to you. What things have always secretly interested you, or have you secretly hoped for, but could not allow yourself to explore? Write them down in your journal as a sort of "to do" or "bucket" list. You are now free to dream – to re-imagine.

Open yourself up to what is possible for you by using your ability to imagine new experiences in different areas of your life. You may now want to re-imagine a new relationship, a new community/tribe, a satisfying way to earn a living, ways to enjoy the freedom you struggled so hard to claim, new ways to express the spiritual or artistic side of yourself – whatever it may be for you. For now, do not worry about *how* you will bring these things into your life, simply concentrate on re-imagining *what* it is you want. We will get to *the how* in a few pages.

This chapter contains practical hacks to help you re-imagine, identify, explore, and honor what you love, what you want, and what you need to do to move forward. You will then learn some easy strategies to make those things into concrete goals and a map for how to achieve them. The tools presented will also help you set your intention about how you want to move forward with your life. You will be introduced (or perhaps reintroduced) to a *mind map, image inspiration collections,* a novel way of using a *flow chart,* and the value of a *personal manifesto.*

As explained earlier, the suggestions and strategies in this book are *not about recovery* from exploitation and/or abuse. Your recovery from the trauma of being robbed of your life by a cult or an abusive domestic situation should be basically complete *before* you consider a reboot. Please don't think of reboot tools and techniques as things that will help with trauma recovery. They are not designed for that. Recovery is about grieving, acknowledging loss and pain, learning to deal with the

challenging emotions that arise due to the trauma, making some meaning of your experience and the resulting losses. A reboot is different. It
is about reclaiming and re-imagining your life in order to move beyond
the trauma and recovery, to create the future you want.

So to continue, imagine what you would like an ideal day of freedom,
fulfilment, and health to look like. Write down what it is you imagine you
would love to do to earn a living. Since you are imagining an ideal day,
why not imagine one using a visual map that is designed in the same
way your creative brain processes and connects ideas – a *mind map*.

By the way, if you feel you are too old now to pursue what you
would have loved to do, consider how you could incorporate elements
or aspects of that love into your life. Yes, some dreams, due to time
or circumstance, become unattainable. By the time I reclaimed my life
it was too late for me to become ... say ... a prima ballerina or pairs
dance skater. So I had to focus on other areas of interest or find a way
to work from the sidelines in one of those fields. I chose to focus on
other areas that were still feasible for me.

One way to explore alternative possibilities for unattainable
dreams is with a mind map.

## MIND MAP:

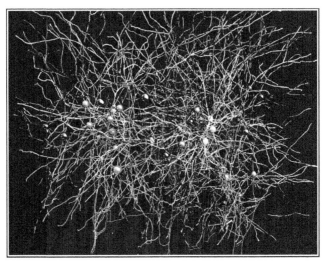

*Image illustrating the brain's neurons and their connective branches*

A mind map is a visual tool that helps explore your thinking on a particular topic – evoking new ideas and connections during the process. It is a form of solitary brainstorming around a core topic. It uses free association rather than a linear list – operating much like the creative right brain, employing hubs of information/ideas with related branches moving out toward other hubs, as illustrated in the image of the brain's neurons above. The point is to explore ... and branch out!

The mind map should be made around a central theme or idea that you want to explore and expand. There will be various paths or branches on your map – some directly related – others more obliquely unrelated. The power of a mind map is that it helps you produce and record ideas and discover relationships among them. New ideas or pathways to achieve them invariably emerge – especially if you let your mind explore without restraint.

Seeing your ideas mapped on paper stimulates the mind and more insights will occur as you work, and even later on after the exercise has awakened the creative right brain. All you need to create a mind map is a pencil and paper.

Write or draw an idea you wish to explore near the middle of a page. (With an 8 1/2" x 11" page, use a landscape orientation with the wider edge along the top). Don't forget to date the page. You can color code the different branches and draw new lines to connect related ideas, if you choose.

Record further ideas related to the central theme (e.g. *how to find work related to dance even if I can no longer be the dancer)* as they occur – even if they don't make sense or seem feasible in the moment. Link ideas that are related (or that build on each other) to the central idea with lines or arrows. Relationships and fresh associations will occur as you work. Suspend judgment. Evaluation can come later – as it does in the brainstorming process. Just free associate for now. Give your mind the simple pleasure of not having to follow rules or make perfect sense. Use as much imagery as you can, employing symbols, drawings, icons, and color.

You do NOT have to be an artist to create a mind map. This is for you and your mind – and your right brain will understand *your* images and appreciate having visual cues that *you* relate to, instead of lists of words favored by your (or someone else's) left brain. No one else needs to understand *your* map unless you decide to share it and explain it. You can always come back to the mind map and add details later. For now what you want are the key topics, subtopics, branches, possibilities, questions, images, and any relationships among them.

If you wish, you can google and find digital templates for mind mapping and download them, but your mind map will probably work best if it just emerges as you re-imagine and explore. Below is an example of a mind map generated from a digital template. It is not a good example of a mind map because, since it has been constructed to instruct, it is very orderly and linear. It basically has a left-brain design before you even start, and once started you are tied to the design. A true mind map is not pre-conceived and laid out so perfectly. That said, this example is provided only to remind you of the key factors to consider when making a mind map.

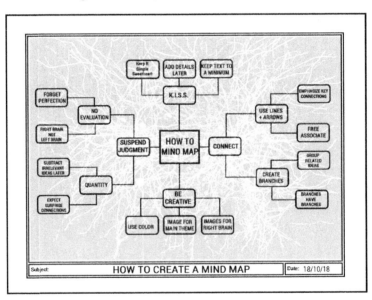

The next image below is an example of a mind map employing all the best suggestions for making one. It is a time-management mind map from *"Mind Map Art"*. Whether you relate to the central theme depicted on it is less important than seeing how this mind map has been constructed. Note how it has many branches coming out of the main hub or trunk of the idea "time management". Images, color (sorry it is in black and white here), arrows and curved lines have been used to activate the creative right brain. Questions have been included related to the exploration. Branches of ideas emanate from other branches. Some had to be squeezed in as the mind came up with them later. That kind of mind map will surely pull you back in later to re-imagine, invent and discover.

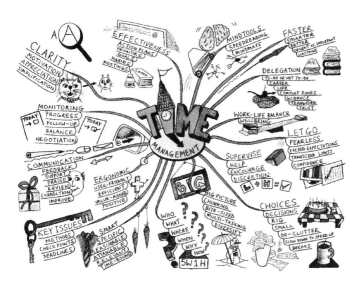

The next image below is what seems to be a hastily constructed mind map, pulled together without the aid of colors or drawings. Even without images and colors that tickle the fancy of the creative right brain, it serves it purpose. It also illustrates how there is no one way or right or wrong way to make a mind map. It can be as rudimentary and unruly as you wish – as long as it is yours.

Mind maps can be elaborate, illustrated explorations, or as below, simple, hand-drawn explorations put to paper to capture all the connections the mind can muster.

The mind map below was created around a central hub of "getting unstuck". You can see many connections were made as the paper filled out until the person hit on an idea that seemed to really excite them. Then the exploration got crowded and messy in upper right corner where that connection was made. The mind map exhibits a different 'character' where they stumbled on the idea of using carpentry skills to build a cottage. Their mind quickly jumps to the ideas of buying land and building a second cottage to sell, and even to creating a cottage building company.

Part of their excitement must come from seeing how the idea of building a cottage connects with several of their other ideas on the mind map such as *using a current skill set, downsizing, learning something new, and canoeing/kayaking/hiking* – and, above all, *getting unstuck*. Yes, one can say that judgments were made when they began to concentrate on the one idea, but it is challenging to not rush to a positive judgment when you discover a viable, exciting connection, so we'll forgive them.

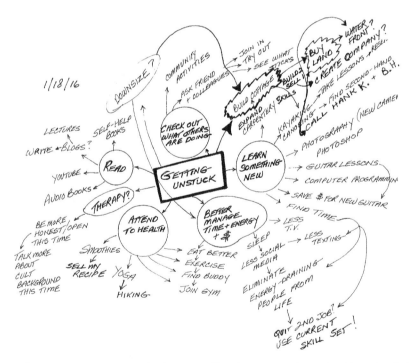

Create your own mind-map allowing your imagination to take flight, letting ideas spill out onto the page. If you think your reboot journal is large enough, you can do mind maps there. Or do one on a separate piece of paper and fold and glue/tuck it into your journal. Work on other mind maps, rewording what you put in the central hub to see if that changes the connections you make.

Again, it is important to try to suspend judgment about what you put on your mind map – at least at first. Do not evaluate the design or how the ideas appear on the page. If you are evaluating as you go, you may end up censoring a key idea that could be just what you need to explore. Look for clues, as in the mind map above, when connection arrows begin to point in one direction. The next mind map for the person above should have "*Build Cottage*" as the central hub and then see what further connections emerge.

Once a mind map seems complete you can go back and re-examine it asking the following questions:

287. How might you inadvertently be mapping your new life by patterning it on someone else's, or on your old, habitual, way of living?

288. How are others' expectations keeping you stuck – defining your life?

289. Does your mind map help you see a way to step out of the old story of your life into a new one – finally of your making? How? What did you discover?

290. How might your wounded, victim child self be sabotaging efforts to change and meet your need to move forward? Is it your child self or your centered adult self that is doing your re-imagining?

291. If you could ask it, what would your future want you to be doing now ... in preparation?

292. Can you spot obstacles to fulfilling any of the important ideas?
  . Create a brainstorming session about how you can overcome that obstacle.

Once you have created and reflected upon a mind map of ideas in a certain area, another strategy that can be a great help is collecting inspiring images related to the subject. Have a place where you gather photos or pictures of dreams, wishes, preferences, activities, environments, etc. that you would like to incorporate into your life. You can, for example, place inspiring images where you will see them frequently such as in your reboot journal. One can imagine the person who created the above mind map collecting images of waterfront land, images and blueprints of cottage designs, construction materials, kayaks, canoes, hiking trails, etc.

## IMAGE INSPIRATION:

Find images that mirror your dreams and excite your imagination. Images can be collected on your computer or in your reboot journal to represent bourgeoning values, hopes, and goals. You can also add text to them that amplifies your hopes for the future, or quotations, or affirmations that inspire you to work toward achieving all or parts of the visual inspiration you collect.

The point is not to lose any of your ideas or intuitions and to have one place where you collect them – a place you go to for inspiration – with visual reminders of what you are working toward. Poet John O'Donohue wrote, *"When you really gaze at something, you bring it inside you."*

Invest in magazines you think might contain images that are related to your dreams. Have fun choosing the images and displaying them – e.g. on pages in your reboot journal. Many of the platforms for storing your own photographs or images gathered on the internet have a collage-making feature where you can assemble relevant images into beautiful arrangements. You can then print them and paste them in your journal.

As you assemble and collage images, it may strike you that many of your images are over-the-top, frivolous, banal or unrelated and you may wonder how you can ever connect them or create a coherent vision of them. Well, you probably can't – at first. A collage of images that pleases you does not have to be coherent or make sense. A collection of image inspiration can hold important pieces of the puzzle of your future – the puzzle of what you want to move toward that, at some serendipitous point, may coalesce into a clear map of not only where you want to go, but also a better vision of how to get there.

Perhaps you have a mental vision of what you want but do not have images to illustrate that vision. Then begin by simply writing down what you envision and would like images for, in your journal. Then keep an eye out for corresponding photographs or images to illustrate each item. Searching for the right images can be an enjoyable part of this exercise.

An image collection could be understood as a sort of compass for your new post-trauma path. A grouping of images will make your dreams more concrete and visible, and will serve as inspiration and even a statement of intention about achieving them. Now I'm not suggesting that whatever you put in your image inspiration collection will magically 'manifest' in your life, as proponents of new-age type ideals believe. But it will be a continual reminder of what you want and what you intend. It cannot be denied you are more likely to bring something into your life that you are reminded of every day than something you never see, envision or contemplate. Images of dreams and goals have pulling power.

Before you identify specific goals, you may want to identify what matters to you now out of the abusive situation – the new values and guiding principles for your life – linking up any associations and related ideas that occur. Make a list of your new guiding principles and the values you aspire to now and with time convert the list into an image inspiration collection.

Then, having collected ideas and having inspiration from your image collection, you may be able to identify specific goals you want to work toward. Once the goal is established, the question always becomes, *"but how do I get from here to there?* If the goal seems like a leap too far, I have an amazing hack for you! With the simple tool of a Barbara Sher *flow chart* you can literally chart out each and every step you need to take to reach your goal. You can learn more about Barbara Sher and her work from her website barbarasher.com.

## FLOW CHART:

A flow chart is a visual aid identifying the sequence of next steps needed to reach a goal. It nails down the path or multiple paths leading straight to the goal. For several years now I have taught many of my clients, who were working toward a challenging goal, the Barbara Sher version of a flow chart. I discovered this form of flow chart in her book, *"Wishcraft: How to Get What You Really Want"*, written with Annie Gottlieb.

Barbara's method is a little counter-intuitive, but brilliant and easy once you get the hang of it. Sher has you write down YOUR GOAL on the right side of the page. On the left side of the page you write "ME". What you fill in between will be the steps to reach your goal. All seems obvious, right? However, when creating a Barbara Sher flowchart you do *not* work from the left (ME) toward the right (GOAL). You do that when you are actually working on achieving the goal. Instead, when making the flow chart of steps, you start on the right at the GOAL and **work backwards** to where you are now (ME). ME ←←←← GOAL

Barbara Sher has you identify the steps you need to take by asking a couple of simple questions as you make the chart. Once the steps to reach the goal are identified, you *then* take the actual steps from ME (where you are now) to your GOAL (where you want to be).

What's exciting is as you construct a flow chart for almost any goal, you will see that the initial steps even toward a very challenging goal, involve non-threatening research or information-gathering. You do not have to dive into any risk-taking steps right away. Here is exactly what you do when making this form of flow chart - fill in the steps (circles) from your goal to where you are now by asking two questions:

**Question #1: Can I do this tomorrow?**

If "*Yes*", do it.

If "*No*", move on to ask question #2.

**Question #2: What would I have to do first?**

Answer and write down on the chart
what you would have to do first.

Looking at what you just wrote, again ask yourself question #1
– "*Can I do this tomorrow?*"

If the answer is "*Yes*", do it.

If the answer is "*No I cannot do this tomorrow*",
then go again to question #2 –

"*What would I have to do first?*" Answer and write it down in front of the
last thing you wrote.

Keep identifying what you would have to do first and write it down. Ask yourself question #1 about each step. Continue this way until you arrive at "ME".

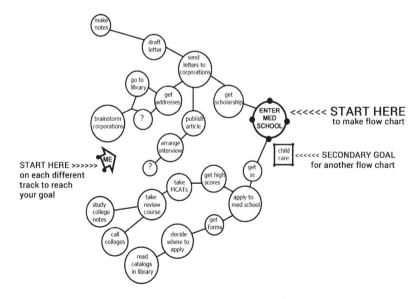

←  ←  ←  Work backwards from goal to where you are now **when making the flow chart**.

→  →  →  Take steps forward toward goal once you have finished flow chart.

In the above flow chart example, the person would keep asking the two questions as follows:

#1. *Can I* **ENTER MED SCHOOL** *tomorrow?* (The answer is "No") so the person asks:

#2. *What would I have to do first?* The answer is "**get in**".

The person writes that down near the goal, and asks:

#1. *"Can I "get in" tomorrow?"* Answer "No".

#2. *What would I have to do first?* The answer is "**apply to med school**".

The person writes that down in front of the last step, and asks:

#1. *Can I apply to med school tomorrow?* The answer is "No"

#2. *What would I have to do first?* The answer is "**get the necessary forms**"

The person writes that down, and asks:

#1. *Can I get the forms tomorrow?* "No" I haven't decided where to apply.

#2. *What would I have to do first?* The answer is "**decide where to apply**".

The person writes that down, and asks:

#1. *Can I decide where to apply tomorrow?* "No"
#2. *What would I have to do first?* Their answer is "**read Med School catalogs in library**"

The person writes that down, and asks:

#1. *Can I read catalogs in library tomorrow?* The answer is "Yes". – **Do it.**

*They now have a starting point and all the next steps on that track to reach the goal of getting into med school.*

As you see from the above flow chart there turns out to be more than one path this person will have to negotiate to "*Enter Med School*". The person asked the same two questions on each separate path until she arrived at where she is today "ME".

As you construct a flow chart, you may see there are other paths related to the goal that will be required. In the one above, the person has noted "*Child Care*" as another goal they will have to work toward in order to go to med school. If you have more than one path of steps to reach your goal, you will have a choice as to which one you want to work on, and when (unless, of course, certain steps have a deadline.) Once you complete the step/s closest to "ME", move to the next step, and so on. You will gain more confidence as you take each step to achieve your goal.

You can easily do your own flow chart by writing Barbara Sher's two questions and instructions at the top of a page and then with your goal on the right and your starting point on the left, proceed from the right – asking the questions – until you reach the left.

Now you have identified your values, vision, goals and the steps needed to reach them, you may want to write something that solidifies your intent and features the guiding principles you will use to achieve what you intend. A personal manifesto can be a powerful statement of your commitment to reclaim your life and a way to confirm what will guide you along the way.

## A PERSONAL MANIFESTO:

While it seems that manifestos have been co-opted by terrorists (such as the "*Unabomber Manifesto*" by Ted Kaczynski) to announce and justify their warped views to the public, manifestos should not only be the domain of disturbed minds.

A manifesto, as described by the Merriam-Webster dictionary, is "*a written statement declaring publicly the intentions, motives, or views of its issuer*". The word "*manifesto*" itself comes from the Latin "*manifestum*" meaning to make clear or conspicuous.

The first record of a manifesto in the English language was in the early seventeenth century. Manifestos are used in many fields: business, education, politics, the arts, science, technology, etc., and in the past were rarely personal. This does not negate, however, the possibility of and value of a personal manifesto.

One amazing public manifesto is the 1955 call to reason about weapons of mass destruction, called the *"Russell-Einstein Manifesto"* by Bertrand Russell and Albert Einstein. Russell described the manifesto as a call to humanity to *"think in a new way"*.

While manifestos have traditionally been public statements and calls to action, you may, for the purpose of getting unstuck want to create a *moving on manifesto*. It can be a personal declaration of values, learnings, wisdom, opinions, principles, intent, goals or purpose.

Manifestos can be a personal call to action – a call to yourself to become the person you want to be – a call to the authentic self you had to hide while being exploited – a call to the part of yourself that will no longer be constrained by past indoctrination, patterns or wounds – a call to yourself to live by new standards and values – a call to reach new heights.

A manifesto should rise above past circumstances and make clear the wisdom you want to inform you now and that you want to make manifest in your life. Using a manifesto as *a touchstone for guiding values and next moves* will help you make decisions and set goals based on *your* ideals rather someone else's.

Writing down your intentions for your new life is a powerful act of self-affirmation, and whether you ever show it to anyone else or not, it will help you focus on your priorities and can make you feel more accountable to demonstrate the intent expressed. A manifesto becomes a mission statement. You could design it to be your personal constitution. Organizational Effectiveness expert, Zach Sumner describes it as *"a form of correspondence with your future self"*.

In an article in Psychology Today, Cathy Malchiodi, Ph.D. says this about making visual representations of our intentions: "*Today, proponents of the value of intention in therapy describe it as a form of **cognitive reframing** and resilience-enhancing behavior. Creating an expression to represent an intention and reinforcing that in regular visual journaling not only serves as a reminder, it is also an imaginal commitment to change…it is possible that when we draw and write about positive* *intentions, we increase the chances of behavior change or at the least establish what we intend in a deeper, more complete manner."*

You can write out, print, or post the *"imaginal commitment"* of your intentions – your manifesto – where you will see it often. Use it as a screen saver on your computer. Keep it in your journal as an affirmation of your intent. Make a poster of it. Make your ideas, principles, intentions and goals visible to inspire yourself. If, down the road, you find your manifesto can serve to inspire others and you want to share it publicly, so much the better.

Go online to find existing manifestos to guide you with this project. You need to get a feel for the typical format and find a style that pleases you. The first two I ever saw before actually creating a few of my own were the *"HOLSTEE Manifesto"* and the *"Lululemon Manifesto"*.

There are as many designs for manifestos as the contents they contain. There are also websites that will guide you through the process of designing a manifesto.

**The Holstee Manifesto** (above right) was written by a Brooklyn-based apparel company of the same name. Its self-help message became so popular it became one of Holstee's bestselling products. An article in The Washington Post in November 2011 by Olga Khazan says the manifesto has been "*... translated into 12 languages, and by Holstee's own approximations, it's been viewed more than 50 million times.*"

The version of the *Holstee* manifesto above has a white background. The page is dense with text which all appears horizontally and uses the same font throughout, in different sizes. Other manifestos contain blank space, text boxes, vertical text, a variety of fonts, different colors, and some include images. The sky is the limit and I hope you will use these examples as a jumpstart for your own ideas. Have fun playing with different ways to present and honor your reboot intentions.

The *Legendary Women Manifesto* (above left) is another example with black background and white text but with different fonts in different sizes. Collect and edit the phrases you want to use and decide exactly how you want to display your words and phrases. There is no right or wrong way. It's your manifesto so make it in a style and format that pleases you.

Some manifestos use an interesting, patterned background with strategically and artfully spaced text throughout. Your text can be hand-written or computer designed using impactful fonts. If you are working in a computer design program, you can also add boxes, lines, and lots of special effects. Be sure to put your name at the bottom with the date and a copyright symbol. If you are like me, it will take a while to get it exactly the way you want it. Enjoy the process.

You could entitle your manifesto something like: "*My Moving On Manifesto*", "*A Post-Trauma Reboot Manifesto*", "*My Personal Constitution*" or "*My Mission Statement*" – whatever. Perhaps you will create more than one – each reflecting different aspects of your values, intent, and goals. The great thing is you can experiment with as many as you want, in whatever way you want. It can be an exciting project that jumpstarts and pulls you forward into the next chapter of your life. Once completed, a manifesto can be used to measure whether choices or activities align with your newly constituted mission statement.

Taking on the project of creating a manifesto is also, by the way, a "new experience" and another wonderful way to rewire your brain after undue coercive controls. You will be giving yourself a challenging experience that pulls you out of a sense of helplessness, making new neural connections that crowd out the old maladaptive ones in the process.

For the purposes of an *"after recovery from trauma reboot"*, begin by noting approximately ten strong, brief, powerful phrases that describe how you want to live your life now that you are free. Write about what you have learned, what matters to you now, the values and principles that will guide you, how you intend to respond to life now, and some aspirations you have for your life.

You can use your reboot journal to sketch out the initial design of your manifesto. Be positive – stating what you want and what you intend, more than what you don't want or don't intend. Positive statements have impact and point the way. The text should inspire and make you want to stretch to attain the ideals they describe. Select brief, punchy statements. Keep editing them down. Remember, it's often what you remove that makes it better! Your personal manifesto will guide, energize and uplift you.

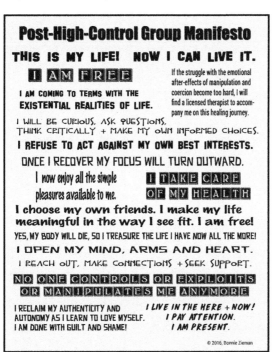

Above is an example manifesto designed for people who have left a high-control group. Viewing posts and comments on Facebook demonstrating how lost, confused, stuck, and alone some cult survivors felt, I hoped a manifesto might encourage them to remember who they are, what their options are once out, and accentuate ways to move forward. I have several manifesto-type posters which you can download without cost on my website bonniezieman.com.

You will find it gratifying to compose, design and produce your own from scratch. Give it a go. You will undoubtedly make several changes and refinements during the design process. Give yourself time to get it right. New ideas will emerge as you work. It becomes a bit like a puzzle, trying to place and fit the phrases you've chosen onto a limited space. And, if like me, you get discouraged in the middle of the process when you encounter blocks, just keep going. Be sure to proofread and edit it carefully, especially if you intend to print it. Based on my experience, it is easy for the designer's eye to overlook small errors.

A manifesto can actually be a significant, long-term guide which will contribute to rebooting your life and to rewiring your brain away from old scripts or neuropathways.

## REVIEW OF METHODS TO HELP RE-IMAGINE YOUR LIFE JOURNEY

- Remember to work on regularly giving yourself new experiences.

- Give yourself *corrective* experiences – happy ones to cancel out the negative ones.

- Learn to practice self-regulation – the ability to manage your emotions and impulses.

- Enjoy frequent moments of quiet time – periods of sweet, incubative silence.

- Gift yourself with the healing practice of journaling.

- Learn and use deep breathing and meditation practices.

- Use guided-imagery to rewire your brain for health, resilience, and calm.

- Cultivate a predominantly *present moment* focus on life.

- Develop a dual focus – of attending to and living in the present moment while at the same time developing a fresh vision for your future.

- Learn how to calm any anxiety by resetting your vagus nerve.

- Read books that support your new way of life and challenge you to reach your potential. (See the Recommended Reading Section at the back of this book.)

- Try different therapeutic modalities.

Remember any time you make your needs, longings, intent, values and goals concrete using mind-maps, image inspiration collections, manifestos, flow charts, etc. you have to leave room for the gifts and grace of serendipity, mystery, and even for temporary detours. It is often in these spaces that "*flow*", "*aha*" moments, or magic happen. As you create these visual supports for reaching your goals, remember details matter. If there is not room for all the details on your mind-map – go in later and fill in details in fine print. Refining the details can be a great help and may point to things you will want to include in your imagery inspiration collection or in your manifesto. Additional steps can always be added to your flow chart.

Your vision for your new life may, at first, be a broad, macro view of the values and environments you want to create for yourself. As you continue this reboot work, your ideas will become more refined and you will be able to fill in more specific details.

Jenny Blake in her book "Pivot: *The Only Move That Matters is Your Next One*" suggests you keep shaping and refining your broad vision and then adds: "... *your ... vision should be so riveting that the thought sends a rush of adrenaline through your body and gets your synapses firing.*" You will be much more inclined to find the energy to work toward a vision that excites you.

## Quotations to Inspire the Need to Re-Imagine:

*"Some journeys are direct, and some are circuitous; some are heroic, and some are fearful and muddled. But every journey, honestly undertaken, stands a chance of taking us toward the place where our deep gladness meets the world's deep need."*
- Parker J. Palmer

*"Do not wait until the conditions are perfect to begin. Beginning makes the conditions perfect."*  -  Alan Cohen

*"Your present circumstances don't determine where you can go. They merely determine where you start."*  -  Nido Qubein

*"A mission statement is not something you write overnight but fundamentally, your mission statement becomes your constitution, the solid expression of your vision and values. It becomes the criterion by which you measure everything else in your life."*
- Stephen Covey

*"After a cruel childhood, one must reinvent oneself. Then reimagine the world."*  -  Mary Oliver

*"Come to the edge," he said.*
*"We can't, we're afraid!" they responded.*
*"Come to the edge," he said.*
*"We can't, we will fall!" they responded.*
*"Come to the edge," he said.*
*And so they came.*
*And he pushed them.*
*And they flew."*

- Guillaume Apollinaire,
French poet/playwright 1880-1918

# 10. RECALIBRATE

Recalibrate definition: *"to readjust precisely for a particular function; to re-determine."* Merriam-Webster

T
O GET UNSTUCK and move forward with your life you will have to reboot from the old corrupt operating system to the new and you will have to find your unique way to do this. A lot of the questions, life hacks and exercises in previous chapters should have already given you a head start on this. Perhaps, if you have already done a lot of personal work, you will just have to refresh the way you look at, think about, and interpret things.

In an unexpected reboot process thrust upon me by writing my memoir, *"Fading Out of the JW Cult"*, the first thing I had to rethink was my belief that all healing work from the indoctrination and exploitation of the JW organization was complete. As I reflected upon my life in and out of the cult and the work done to recover, it soon became clear that even all these years later I could benefit from reconsidering and recalibrating some of my habitual defenses – denial, avoidance, suppression, and/or somatization (somatization is unexplained physical symptoms due to unconscious psychological factors). They were getting in the way of some of my practical, real life goals.

Although I had paid occasional nods to the possibility I had been somatizing psychological distress since childhood – I tended to conveniently forget (unconsciously repress) the possibility of

148 | BONNIE ZIEMAN

somatization and with the appearance of an ailment would just cope, live with it, use alternative techniques to deal with it, or occasionally seek out professional health care.

Reviewing my life while writing the memoir made me realize that frequent mysterious ailments might very well have been my body speaking to me about unresolved feelings, unaddressed inner conflicts, and/or buried pain or anger. *Or*, the physical ailments were perhaps my body's way of trying to release feelings I had denied or repressed – or at the very least its effort to get me to turn my attention to them. As well, with all the work I had already done, I now had healthier ego strength and the old defense measures were not as essential and could be let go.

Timothy Butler in his book "*Getting Unstuck*" says, "*When a life crisis or impasse shakes things up, it weakens the defensive structures we have built up to repel aspects of being that, for whatever reason, we had unconsciously labeled as "not me". With these defenses weakened, we find ourselves with the opportunity to live a part of ourselves that had been left behind.*"

The 'crisis' of going over my past with a fine tooth comb for the memoir seemed to relax my default defensive structures of repression and somatization – at the very least it made me reflect upon them. Then I was able to address them in more depth than I had before and actually begin to recalibrate old defensive habits.

Your review and re-assessment of your old, coercively-controlled life and getting free should provide insights and some clear next steps for you too!

But before we recalibrate or readjust anything we have to have an idea of how exactly defensive strategies work – of what represents optimal psychological functioning and what does not. We especially want to recalibrate the operating system learned in situations of manipulation, exploitation, or abuse. Let's look at one model of the psyche's basic operating system that can help us to understand it.

## FREUD'S MODEL OF THE PSYCHE

Just as I am using the analogy of rebooting a computer throughout this book to help explain how to reset patterns of thought and action that result from trauma, the founder of psychoanalysis Sigmund Freud, an Austrian neurologist used a representation of the psyche that can help explain some of the inner dynamics at play in any human. Freud's theoretical model will be used here to describe and understand the inner tendencies at work after any traumatic situation. Freud proposed that there are three different energies, components, or functions active in every human psyche. He labelled these representations the **Ego**, the **Superego**, and the **Id**.

Just as we do not actually have a computer operating in our psyche but it serves as a useful analogy for describing inner processes that can keep us stuck in certain behavior patterns, so too there is no *actual* Ego, no *literal* Superego, or *actual* Id laboring in our psyche. They are simply convenient terms to describe certain *functions* of the psyche. Whether one subscribes to Freud's model of psychodynamic therapy or not, one can still benefit from using his model of the components or energies that make up the human psyche. We will use Freud's model of these three functions to help better understand why we may be stuck, what dynamics might be at play, and what we need to do to get unstuck. Here is a brief description of these functions of the psyche:

**EGO**: The ego is a name and description used in Freudian theory to illustrate the part of the personality each human presents to the world and identifies as "self". It is the part of the psyche that perceives the world and interprets what it perceives. It is the function that determines what is needed, makes decisions and takes actions to fulfill those needs. Egos are often described as operating on a fragile to strong continuum. Fragile egos are often protected by "ego defenses" (denial, avoidance, repression, etc.) until they are strong enough to deal with the reality that threatens. The ego tries to ensure survival by keeping us safe. A strong, healthy ego is one that can manage stress, regulate emotions, solve problems, and react to life's challenges with resilience.

**SUPEREGO**: The superego is not the conscience, but rather develops from parental introjects (internalizations) and holds and tries to administer rules, inhibitions and injunctions from the past. With development, maturity, and self-awareness the superego loses control over an ego that becomes more and more autonomous (less in need of the parental or god-like voice to tell it how to behave). When normal development is stalled, the superego can continue to control our beliefs, perceptions and behaviors. People raised in high-control environments will have likely internalized the interdictions of the group as part of their superego. Their task is then to become aware of the superego's harsh voice and free themselves of its trauma-mirroring tyranny. The goal is for the ego function to develop an identity inde-pendent of harsh superego influences. The harsh part of the superego strives for perfection. Once we tame the harsh voice of the superego, its supportive voice should reappear.

**ID**: The instinctual impulses of the Id part of the psyche are con-stantly being influenced by the Ego and the Superego. Freudian theory says the Id looks for pleasure and immediate gratification. "*In Freudian theory, the division of the psyche that is totally unconscious and serves as the source of instinctual impulse and demands for immediate satis-faction of primitive needs.*" - Gregory Mitchell.

## THE INNER CRITIC or HARSH SUPEREGO

One of the main things we have to release after leaving a high-control, traumatic situation is our inner critic. This is the inner voice that finds fault with our behaviours, ideas, and often our very self. Therapists still sometimes use the word Freud coined for the inner critic – the "super-ego". Transactional therapists refer to this part of the psyche as the "inner parent" instead of the inner critic. It is the judgmental, parent-like, even god-like voice telling us we are not good enough.

While the superego is concerned about our moral appearance and reputation, it is not the conscience. Rather, the superego originates with parental, religious, and cultural internalizations and contains inhi-bitions and injunctions from those systems and from the past.

With development, maturity, and self-awareness the harsh super-ego (inner parent) should lose its controlling power over an ego (the adult function of the self) that becomes more and more autonomous (less in need of the parental or 'god-like' voice inside to tell it how to behave). With maturity the superego can eventually become a support to the healthy, strong, independent ego – cheering for it like a healthy parent, rather than criticizing it.

When normal development is stalled, for whatever reason, or when/if we regress to feeling childlike in the midst of traumatic experiences, the harsh voice of the superego can jump in to try to exercise strict dominance over our perceptions and behavior.

People raised in a cult-like, high-control environment will have internalized the rules and interdictions of the controlling group as part of the voice of their superego or inner critic. Their task is then to become aware of the harsh superego's input and to free themselves of that tyrannical, chastising, inhibitive voice.

The goal is for the healthy adult ego to develop an identity independent of harsh superego influences, demands, and reprimands. Ben Ringler, MFT, in his book *"Good Therapy"* gives us a good description of the superego:

*"Have you ever thought, "I'm my own worst enemy"? Do you ever feel plagued by a relentlessly critical internal voice? Perhaps you feel stuck and find it difficult to think creatively about how to overcome challenges in your life. Even if you have a plan to address challenges, you might still find it difficult to take action. If you find yourself experiencing these or other negative thoughts and feelings frequently, you may be dealing with a harsh superego.*

*"This internal "enemy" is the voice in our heads that reminds us of our failings and shortcomings. It reprimands us when we think or act independently of its proscribed behaviour, and it can censor us in very sneaky ways. At times, it may be almost like living under the shadow of an intimidating, abusive parent... a harsh superego can make it feel like there is an internal someone or something that is intent on destruction.*

*"Those who experience this harshness, these internal cuts, might often feel stuck in life."*

*Illustration of Freud's three different symbolic
representations of the psyche*

To repeat, while the voice of the superego can be supportive, it is often a harsh, demanding, punitive, inner critic and it is important not to interpret the harsh voice of the inner critic as the voice of our conscience. They are two very different things.

Timothy Butler goes on to tell us *"The super-ego is not the conscience; it is not moral, it is not the "small, still voice" of the Bible. Rather it is "the loudest voice within us", and its concern is not to redress wrongs or take moral action; its concern is to punish and stop us from taking that action which would allow us to experience new possibilities."*

If you need to remove the crushing presence of a harsh superego's voice in your head, you must begin by noticing when it is there. You must start to name its statements for what they are: inaccurate, distorted, sometimes cruel, often punitive, and certainly unhelpful. Remind yourself that this harsh voice infantilizes you, judges you, discourages you, tries to make you toe the line, and can keep you stuck. Remind yourself that you are now an adult and do not need controlling supervision by the superego or inner critic.

Your superego's voice may be difficult to differentiate from the voice of the cult and its leaders – or the voice of demanding or abusive parents. It is definitely not the voice of your higher self. It is possible your superego is sabotaging your movement forward into your new life because it does not like the fact that you abandoned cult and/or family values, beliefs, and ways of living.

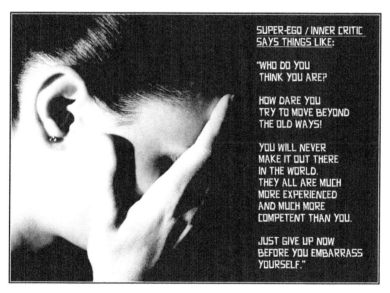

SUPER-EGO / INNER CRITIC SAYS THINGS LIKE:

"WHO DO YOU THINK YOU ARE?

HOW DARE YOU TRY TO MOVE BEYOND THE OLD WAYS!

YOU WILL NEVER MAKE IT OUT THERE IN THE WORLD. THEY ALL ARE MUCH MORE EXPERIENCED AND MUCH MORE COMPETENT THAN YOU.

JUST GIVE UP NOW BEFORE YOU EMBARRASS YOURSELF."

The harsh superego is a primitive, arcane voice that must be put in its place. *Name it as irrelevant, outdated, and unreasonable.* Tell it you do not believe what it says and will not adjust your behaviors or goals to accommodate its outdated views. Tell it to be quiet. Tell it: *"Enough!"*

Also if you can, try to notice what you are doing or thinking when this judgmental voice appears. You are probably doing something that excites you, but that threatens the superego's control over you, or threatens what it believes will be your standing with the groups or people it wants you to model yourself after. The harsh superego often 'attacks' right when you want to take a step into a new experience that will enrich your life. You must be firm and dismiss it if you want to move forward. A few life hacks to do just that follow.

*"Tell that imperious voice in your head to be still."* - Barbara Kingsolver

## STRUGGLING WITH INNER CRITIC or SABOTEUR ENERGIES

Many physical ailments throughout my life were actually a defense against having to do things I did not want to do. With some reflection while writing my memoir, I realized my superego knew I no longer listened to its criticism and it would have to radically change its tactic in order to control me. It did so by using physical ailments and/or pain, rather than inner criticism. This way it could accomplish one of three goals:

- *punish* me for moving past the limits prescribed for me by my family or the cult

- *prevent* me from doing things that would further alienate me from my family

- *protect* me from doing things that raised my anxiety and (according to it, things that could 'ruin' my reputation) – even if they were things I really wanted to do now.

This somatizing pattern (psyche creating ailments in body) that I had enabled as a teenager to get out of going to cult meetings or proselytizing door-to-door, had now morphed into an annoying, autonomous pattern.

If you have been plagued with mysterious pain or ailments, you may want to consider if they might be caused by the harsh superego as an effort to *punish*, *distract*, *prevent* or *protect* you from an action it considers beyond previously established norms, or out-of-bounds.

Of course, sometimes a headache is just a headache. But having survived the harsh controls of a coercive family or group it is not outrageous to consider your strict superego might be using illness, pain, or other forms of self-sabotage such as accidents, mistakes, failures, stuckness, forgetfulness, depression, etc. to try and keep you tied to those old rules or to punish you for breaking them. I recommend books (See Recommended Reading section at the back of this book for titles) by John Sarno, M.D., and Eckhart Tolle to help free yourself from any debilitating pattern of sabotage and/or somatization.

## LIFE HACKS TO STRENGTHEN THE HEALTHY EGO & REDUCE THE POWER OF THE SUPEREGO

As you gift yourself with new life experiences you will be strengthening your healthy, adult ego and with good ego strength you will be better able to silence the voice of the inner critic or harsh superego. Gregory Mitchell, author of "Ego Autonomy and Overcoming the Superego", says:

*"The Ego can only become truly Autonomous by overcoming the Superego. The Autonomous Ego, by and large is free from the dictates of the Id and has outgrown the Superego. The Ego understands and has integrated the energetic drives of the Id and sublimates them toward loving sexuality and creative activity. The Autonomous Ego creates his or her own moral code and relies on his or her own sense of right and wrong, based on rational and objective analysis. This is an Independent Mind."*

If you persistently feel stuck, it may be that you have a harsh superego interfering with your independent choices, discouraging you, sabotaging you, and holding you back. A healthy, autonomous ego is what you want for yourself now. It is the autonomous, adult ego state that will set limits on the interference of the superego/inner critic and help you get unstuck.

With a strong, independent ego you will be able to easily identify the voice of your inner critic, name it as not acting in your best interests, and dismiss it. When bullies are exposed they often weaken and back off. So too with the bullying superego. To identify its interference you have to have educated yourself about it and watch for its sneaky appearance when you least want it.

Ben Ringler, MFT, in an article *"Breaking the Chains: Finding Relief from a Harsh Superego"* on his website "**Good**Therapy" offers valuable suggestions on how to do this: *"The central vehicle for change is awareness. The more you are aware of the harsh superego, the more empowered you are to change it. There are practices you can employ at home that are often helpful. I suggest a daily meditation practice of 5-10 minutes. Focus on the breath and observe all manifestations of the harsh superego as they arise.*

- *Notice how audible it is. Does it yell? Whisper? Is this voice familiar?*

- *Notice its particular brand of harshness. Does it criticize you? Shame you? Berate you?*

- *Notice what it focuses its attention on: Not "doing it right"? Your intelligence? Appearance? Level of success?*

- *Notice how it might work on you in silent ways.*

- *Notice how you relate to it. Do you cower in response? Feel tight in your body? Feel angry or anxious?*

*These are all important things to consider as you become more aware of the harsh superego, in order for you to catch it at increasingly earlier stages and lessen its negative impact."*

The voice of my superego would make an appearance each time I began to write a new book about how to recover from JW abuses. My superego was apparently threatened by any seeming public rebuke of the JW organization, because it apparently still believed all the antiquated cult beliefs and rules – and wanted me to toe the line too. It may also have hoped to help me stay 'safe' and connected by not further alienating my devout JW family with my writing.

When you move beyond the abusive situation, speak out against it, or create a new life counter to its tenets, you can be sure superego judgments and interdictions will pop up to try and hold you back. You have to discern the particular strategy of *your* superego. You have to catch it in the act. Document its interference in your reboot journal. Tell it you know what it is doing and you will not be controlled or sabotaged. Dismiss it. Above all, forge ahead with your new values, beliefs, choices, and goals in spite of its interference. The best life hack for you to get unstuck might be the rejection of the voice of the harsh superego.

## QUESTIONS ABOUT YOUR HARSH SUPEREGO:

293. Is your own inner critic or superego doing its best to keep you stuck in the old, abusive paradigm? Explain how you think this might be so.

294. How can *you* specifically use the above techniques to silence the superego?

295. What self-assessments or self-judgments need to be subtracted from your life?

296. Do you need to release a mind-set that always tells you what is not possible?

297. Are you able to identify ways your superego has you sabotage yourself – especially when you try to move forward with your life? Name them. Develop ways to counteract them. Write about all of this in your reboot journal.

## HEALTHY EGO AND RESILIENCE

One of the best ways to reboot your life is to work on developing a healthy ego that can tolerate the voice of the inner critic – one that is resilient in the face of attacks from within and without. What does a healthy ego look like? Your ego is healthy when, among other things, you are:

- optimistic
- resourceful, responsible
- compassionate
- authentic
- adaptive, flexible
- able to love and be loved

- convinced you are deserving

- open to opposing points of view

- enjoying a sense of personal power

- able to tolerate discomfort

- not overwhelmed by triggers

- able to manage difficult emotions

You develop traits like these by being an active participant in life. The more experiences you afford yourself, the more opportunity your ego has to learn, strengthen, grow and bounce back from whatever life hands it. Once you can say you have developed most of the above traits you will be able to recalibrate your life and move forward with your own goals.

The encouraging thing is that the fact you worked up the courage to leave an abusive situation and suffer all the repercussions for so doing demonstrates you already have a significant degree of ego strength and resilience! Gever Tulley says, *"Persistence and resilience only come from having been given the chance to work through difficult problems."* Many of the suggestions, questions, exercises and tools provided in this book are in service of recalibrating your ego strength and developing resilience. If you commit to employing them, as opposed to simply reading them, you will restore your sense of resilience and competence.

You are resilient when you enjoy a sense of autonomy, are able to adapt, have a sense of competence, are able to problem-solve, are able to absorb stress, are able to tolerate anxiety, are able to regulate emotions and, like the flower in this image, are able to bounce back and grow by blooming where you're planted. If you do not yet feel resilient, you need to consciously work on developing the above listed qualities. You can best do that by gifting yourself with new experiences.

## Quotations to Help Quiet the Inner Critic:

*"Strong people alone know how to organize their suffering so as to bear only the most necessary pain."* - Emil Dorian

*"If your compassion does not include yourself, it is incomplete."* - Buddha

*"If you gave your inner genius as much credence as your inner critic, you would be light years ahead of where you now stand."* - Alan Cohen

*"The sky will bow down to your beauty, if you do."* - Rumi

# 11. REVISIT & REFRESH

Revisit definition: *"to consider again especially with the possibility of change or reversal"*; Refresh Definition: *"to bring back to a former condition or vigor"* Merriam-Webster

W E ALL, AS my own story reveals, have to revisit and reconsider our habits, patterns and default responses – throughout life. We may have done considerable work to recover from the abuse of deception, manipulation, exploitation and abuse and then presume the work is done.

Healing and growth however, occur like a spiral where we cycle back around and past previous work – and begin again. But the next cycle is working on our development at a higher level. This is *not* evidence of not having worked hard enough in the past. It is how development, learning, growth, and healing manifest.

*"We have learned so much … there still remains much to learn. We are not going in circles, we are going upwards. The path is a spiral; we have already climbed many steps."* - Herman Hesse, *Siddhartha*

With that in mind, when we find ourselves "stuck" after recovery from trauma, it may be we are being invited by life to revisit (spiral back around) our personal patterns of thinking and our habitual responses to blockages or problems.

In this chapter we will look at ways to revisit a few topics you have probably already addressed – but we will do so at a different level on the spiral of growth. A few topics will be re-introduced and then you will be offered questions to help you revisit, reassess, and refresh your relationship to the subject matter. Let's begin.

## REVISIT & REFRESH YOUR RELATIONSHIP WITH FEAR OF PAIN

Psychologist, Rick Hanson developed a three-step model that illuminates an internal dynamic that can cause one to end up stuck. He says a natural impulse for self-expression arises but is soon sabotaged by an expectation of pain (in the form of anticipation of rejection, feeling stupid, being abandoned, getting wounded, being disappointed, being humiliated or shamed, etc.). In order to thwart this knee-jerk expectation of emotional pain, if we dare to express or act on our own behalf, we unconsciously drag out defenses or self-protective measures against pain. These defensive strategies hinder our ability to move forward with life. Anticipation of pain awakens fear and/or anxiety. Humans often take that fear or anxiety as a signal to stop what they are doing.

All of this happens at an unconscious level and is completed before we are even aware of it. The actual defenses can be dramatic or minimal – from getting angry with self or others, running away, avoiding, claiming we do not really want to take that risk after all, making jokes about what a silly idea it is, feeling paralyzed, self-sabotaging, getting sick, etc.

Rick Hanson tells those of us who find ourselves caught in the above-described fear-based "stuck cycle", that it is an opportunity for growth *if* we consciously and gently work with the automatic fear defense to avoid pain. He says,

"... *gradually, in a very step-by-step, careful way, ... take managed risks of the dreaded experience from the inside out (helping yourself) or from the outside in (drawing on others, therapists or coaches, to help in taking those risks.)*"

You can refresh your life by being willing to *"take managed risks"* in spite of any anxiety that accompanies the impulse to try something new. Don't take the anxiety or fear as a signal to stop, but rather as a signal that you are moving into new territory and need to pay attention. Creating and following a flow chart, as demonstrated in a previous chapter, is one technique that will help you take managed risks on the way to any goal.

## QUESTIONS ABOUT ANTICIPATING PAIN:

298.   What pain do you fear if you dare to step forward and express your authentic self?

299.   What typical defenses do you use to protect yourself from the expectation of pain?

300.   Is it possible that it is those very defenses against the expectation of pain that are keeping you stuck?

301.   How might you begin to *"take managed risks"* to help yourself move forward in spite of the expectation of pain?

302.   Would you be willing to ask Byron Katie's four questions ("1. Is it true? 2. Can you absolutely know it's true? 3. How do you react, what happens, when you believe that thought? 4. Who would you be without the thought? *Then*, turn the statement around.") with regard to your expectation of pain when you dare to act on your own behalf?

*"There is no sin punished more implacably by nature than the sin of resistance to change."* - Anne Morrow Lindbergh

*"Life does not accommodate you, it shatters you ... Every seed destroys its container or else there would be no fruition."* - Florida Scott-Maxwell

## REVISIT & REFRESH YOUR RELATIONSHIP WITH GUILT

Guilt is feeling responsibility and remorse for something we have done. In any life some guilt will be felt and can be appropriate. *Guilt for errors or wrongdoing* needs to be addressed by making amends and/or apologizing.

Some guilt, however, is deliberately cultivated by others such as parents or groups (and can even be prompted internally by the superego), in order to better control us. When that guilt persists, it is neurotic — untrue, unnecessary and counterproductive.

Part of stepping up in life now is recognizing you are *not* guilty if you do not conform to rules imposed by an outside source, inner critic, or misguided parent. You alone are responsible for how you constitute your life now. A healthy, resilient ego is not plagued by neurotic guilt.

It is now your job to reject any imposed, outdated, *neurotic guilt* and any accompanying unconscious wish, need, expectation, or belief in a need for punishment that often results from feelings of neurotic guilt. Based on the old, deeply imbedded, Biblical template, guilt almost always demands punishment, inside our own psyche. If the superego thinks we are guilty or senses the ego feels guilty, it will get busy concocting a way to punish us using depression, self-sabotage, accidents, illness, pain, stuckness, etc.

Another form of guilt can be felt due to having abdicated, or been thwarted from meeting, our responsibility to reach our innate potential. We are rarely aware of this reason for a vague sense of guilt and we may, therefore, ascribe the guilt to something else.

This form of guilt — *existential guilt* — is actually a signal from our unconscious that we have not stepped up to meet the possibilities or promise of our individual existence. When we don't understand the guilt as a signal, the pervasive sense of guilt itself may further hinder us from meeting our potential. To repeat, existential guilt is feeling guilty because we were not able, or did not accept personal responsibility to fulfil our unique potential.

Existential guilt is often more about what *you have not done*, than what you have done. (There is an entire chapter in *Exiting the JW Cult: A Healing Handbook*, 2015 that explains the different ways we may experience guilt once out of the cult – and what to do about it.) Your guilt might be because you have not (for whatever reason) stepped up to meet the opportunities offered by life. Once you are free to assume responsibility to meet your potential *and you do*, that form of guilt will be unnecessary and should fade away. Not living your life as fully as you can, often leads to alienation from the self, anxiety, despair, paralysis, and guilt. Sorting this out for yourself can produce tremendous relief and the energy to move forward with life.

Relief from existential guilt comes from taking responsibility for where you are in your life and from taking actions to become fully engaged with life. The guilt does not just recede once you finally "meet your potential". (Few if any of us actually ever know when that moment happens!) It recedes as you actively engage with life to fulfil your potential. Being an active participant in life will increase your self-confidence and self-respect and diminish, if not extinguish, any existential guilt.

It is not enough to become aware of the need to accept responsibility for the state of your life. You must assume responsibility by taking action on behalf of yourself. However, Yalom tells us, "*One can only act for oneself if one has access to one's desires.*" The life hacks and questions in this book should help you access and attend to the needs, wants, dreams, and desires that had to be set aside and free you up to work toward finally claiming your right to fulfill your potential.

## QUESTIONS ABOUT YOUR RELATIONSHIP TO GUILT:

303.   How are you crippled or stalled because of guilt?

304.   Has your harsh superego pronounced you guilty of abandoning God, truth, your family, and of breaking their rules? How does that affect you?

305. How might *your* superego sense guilt and demand punishment, taking the form of self-sabotage, failure, accidents, depression, physical illness, avoidance, staying stuck, etc.?

306. How can you use the above information to recalibrate and reduce the amount of guilt you feel?

307. Can you acknowledge any guilt holding you back probably originates with parental or cult beliefs designed to control you, and is, therefore, now irrelevant?

308. Can you commit to reminding yourself that feelings of guilt often arise because you have not seized the reins of your life in order to meet your potential?

309. Can you reflect on moments when you are consumed by guilt and determine if they emerge and coincide with times you feel good, excited, or ready to take on a new challenge? (What a cruel form of self-sabotage.)

310. Could it be your harsh superego/inner critic is holding you back from activities it does not approve of, by making you feel unworthy or guilty?

311. How might you have colluded with your superego in sabotaging goals and plans?

312. Have you unconsciously decided that, due to your past, you are not worthy of moving forward and enjoying your life? Do you see how this may please the harsh superego?

313. Do you feel creating a new life will be disloyal to those you had to leave behind in the coercive control situation? Explain and challenge such beliefs or feelings.

314. Was there a family imperative (unstated expectation) that you *not* surpass the level of success your parents attained? Explain and challenge that unfair imperative.

315. Can you take time to find something you feel good about and try to expand the feeling in your body/mind? Use this exercise to crowd out the guilt when it rears its ugly head.

316. Can you commit to refusing to allow the inner critic to dominate your consciousness – and thereby – your actions and life?

317. Can you shine the light of awareness on the inner critic in your life? Inner critics, like bullies, usually back off when exposed.

318. What would you be doing now if you were not encumbered by the nay-saying of your inner critic?

319. Can you refuse to let things you are not good at define you? *"...if you judge a fish by its ability to climb a tree, it will live its whole life believing that it is stupid."* - Albert Einstein

320. Can you work to remember all of who you are now – all you have survived – all you have learned, all that you are?

321. What do you need to do to reclaim all of who you are – the parts of you that had to be suppressed to survive the trauma and/or abuse?

322. Can you make the shift into your healthy, autonomous, authentic adult self? Perhaps you have to reconfirm your sense of authentic identity, sense of competence, and sense of self-esteem since leaving everything behind after trauma. Again, therapy will speed up your work on any of this. Providing yourself with corrective experiences which are full of opportunities to build identity, competence and self-esteem will also be pivotal in helping you move forward.

*"Through loyalty to the past, our mind refuses to realize that tomorrow's joy is possible only if today's makes way for it; that each wave owes the beauty of its line to the withdrawal of the receding one."* - Andre Gide

*"What is it that you need to unlearn ... what is it time for you to let go of? ... what chapter of your life is over now?"* - William Bridges

*"The greatest fear that human beings experience is not death, which is inevitable, but consideration of the distinct possibility of living a worthless life."* - Kilroy J. Oldster

*"There is something infantile in the presumption that somebody else has a responsibility to give your life meaning and point. The truly adult view, by contrast, is that our life is as meaningful, as full and as wonderful as we choose to make it."* - Richard Dawkins

## REFRESH YOUR EFFORTS AT EMOTIONAL SELF-CARE:

If you realize you still have a lot of emotional healing to do and that you will keep feeling "stuck" and unable to move forward, you may want to work through the unresolved issues and feelings in therapy. You may also want to examine if you neglect nourishing self-care. Often what provides emotional comfort are simple acts of care with or for the body. Here are a few questions worth considering about your attention to emotional self-care:

323. What do you do to replenish, restore and relax?

324. When you have a day to yourself, do you make time for sweet, simple acts of emotional self-care? What exactly?

325. Do you take quiet walks in nature?

326. Do you make time to sit quietly and mindfully observe the environment around you?

327. Have you learned how to practice mindfulness?

328. Do you listen to guided meditations that relax your body and ease your mind?

329. What things do you consistently do to help support your body/mind through any emotional ups and downs? What more can you add to this list?

What you are looking for is a balance between self-care, regulation of feelings, and active steps into your new life. It takes time, patience and compassion to develop such a balance.

The books, lectures and meditations on YouTube of teacher and author, Tara Brach can be a great help to relax into your trauma-recovered life. Linda Graham in her book, *"Bouncing Back"*, tells us: *"Imaginative exercises [guided imagery] actually change the neural circuitry of our brains, creating new, positive habits of mind that become genuine resources in coping with anything, anything at all."*

Remember that as you refresh and recalibrate, demands for constant perfection, perfect ease, or total comfort will impede your ability to change, grow and recover. You do not have to wait to feel completely healed, recovered, or comfortable to take steps to get on with your life.

Few things are either/or situations e.g. *"I can only work on my future and release my past if I feel fully recovered from all my wounds".* That is rarely the case. People who have suffered great losses can still (and are) creating meaningful lives for themselves – especially when they make a point to care for their physical and emotional well-being as they create a new life.

## MORE QUESTIONS:

330.  How are you insisting on perfect answers, immediate healing results, or absolute safety before you can move on with your life? Describe and challenge.

331.  How have you unconsciously set limits on what you can attempt, how far you can go, what you are allowed to do, how much you can succeed? Describe and challenge.

332.  Can you look at your current situation (e.g. your grief) as the starting point for new life instead of the barrier to it?

333.  How might you be cut off from your own guidance or original operating system?

334.  How might a habit of worrying be getting in your way? Describe and challenge.

335.  Are regrets and resentments keeping you stuck? Describe and challenge.

336.  Have you considered that working on forgiveness of yourself and others may be the key to getting unstuck?

337.  How could you add some quiet, silence, and contemplative time

to your life to help you tap into the knowing of your inner self about what you need to do next?

338. Based on what you know about yourself and have learned in this book, what do you need to do differently – right now?

339. Can you use your desires as one guide as to how to move ahead?

340. While wanting to reconstruct a new life, how have you limited decisions or actions that would help accomplish that desire?

## QUESTIONS ABOUT REVISITING & REFRESHING YOUR RELATIONSHIP WITH TIME:

341. How is a simple thing like time management keeping you from moving forward?

342. Where and how do you mismanage your time?

343. What do you need to do less, in order to accomplish more?

344. How do you spend time on things to distract you from your emotional pain?

345. Who are the people who monopolize your time and drain you of your energy?

346. What are a few simple adjustments you can make now to give yourself more time to work on your healing, work on your goals, and give yourself new experiences?

347. Are you aware that when you better manage your time you increase the energy you have available to achieve goals?

The point here is not to develop stressful feelings that there is not enough time, or that there is some urgency to accomplish your goals. We each need to remember that time is an artificial construct – one we have to adapt to in order to live in this modern world. We need to manage our time but not be governed by the thought of *"never enough time"*.

I like to remind myself that the present moment is actually eternal – and when I feel pressured, I simply bring myself back into present moment awareness. I can only do what I am doing in this moment. I can only do one thing at a time and if that thing is worth my life energy I will give it all of my attention. If it is not, I will let it go. A similar approach could help you too.

This kind of more mindful approach takes so much pressure off. The time you have is the time you have. The exciting thing is you no longer have a controlling organization or family system telling you how you must use your time. Now you decide.

## A Few Quotations About the Mystery of Time:

*"Time isn't made up of discrete moments that pass out of the present and into the past. Time is an endless flow of experience that never stops being now."* - Steve Taylor, PhD

*"All that really belongs to us is time; even he who has nothing else has that."* - Baltasar Gracian

*"Time is a created thing. To say "I don't have time", is like saying "I don't want to".* - Lao Tzu

*"The trouble is, you think you have time."* - Buddha

*"Your time is limited, so don't waste it living someone else's life."* - Steve Jobs

*"The bad news is time flies. The good news is you're the pilot."* - Anonymous

## REVISIT & REFRESH HABITUAL PATTERNS OF THINKING

Just as giving yourself new experiences will help rewire your brain away from the repressive and delusional teachings you had to believe and practice in a high-control milieu, so too developing a new way of thinking and new thoughts will replace some of the old scripts, stories, programming and wiring from the past. Sometimes you are just not aware of how often you engage in the same old, negative train of thought. Are you like a train stuck on its track – stalled in a limited point of view that prevents you from opening up to possibilities that surround you?

Eckhart Tolle tells us, *"Once you have identified with some form of negativity, you do not want to let it go, and on a deeply unconscious level, you do not want positive change. It would threaten your identity as a depressed, angry or hard-done by person. You will then ignore, deny or sabotage the positive in your life. This is a common phenomenon. It is also insane."* Does negativity have a hold on you? Does a negative mind-set make you unconsciously sabotage what could be positive in your life?

We are often stalled in our movement forward in life by cognitive distortions - which are beliefs that create negative moods or mindsets. Pessimism, black and white thinking, overgeneralization, catastrophizing are patterns of thought that distort reality. See The Appendix for a more comprehensive list of *cognitive distortions*.

You can recalibrate any distorted thinking keeping you stuck by engaging in what psychologists call *"cognitive restructuring"* – literally training yourself to think differently. As you do so, you will rewire your brain to see possibilities, where before it could only see the limitations or negatives in any situation. To help with cognitive restructuring I encourage you to read: *"The Brain's Way of Healing"*, by Norman Doidge, M.D., and *"Rewire Your Brain"* by John B. Arden, Ph.D.

Timothy Butler says, *"Mental models tamp a lot down, keeping information out of our awareness. What we need then is a means for temporarily suspending our mental models so we can let … feelings, images, and instincts drift up again. The first step is to find a way to break our conditioned habits of thinking … "*

One excellent way to break up your conditioned habits of thinking and restructure your limiting cognitions is to create affirmations (corrective thoughts) to replace thinking that keeps you from moving forward with your new life. What is an affirmation? Merriam-Webster Dictionary says, among other things, that an affirmation is simply *"a positive assertion"*.

When creating positive assertions (cognitive restructuring), you want to compose statements reflecting your new values that pull your thinking away from any fear, guilt and negativity. Positive affirmations can also be used to cognitively restructure self-sabotaging thoughts that keep you stuck. Thoughts such as: *"I'm too far behind to catch up"*, *"I could never do that"*, *"I never know where or how to start"*, *"I always end up disappointed"*, etc.

You can create affirmations to counter habitual cognitive distortions and jumpstart your movement forward – away from all the corrupted files previously driving your behavior. Choose a couple of affirmations from the following list and repeat them frequently.

## A few affirmations you can use to reboot your thinking:

- Recovery is a process of two steps forward, one step back. I am proud of my progress

- Although there may be setbacks, I love how I now have the courage to stand up for myself.

- Even when I find myself at an impasse, I accept, love and forgive myself.

- I refuse to be held back by regret, anger, or guilt about my past.

- I allow no one to place limits on my abilities and possibilities.

- I am patient with my progress.

- Being human can be a messy, unpredictable business, and I can cope.

- I treat myself with love and compassion as I adjust to freedom.

- I am always good enough.

- I am learning to turn toward my difficulties rather than hiding from them.

- I refuse to criticize myself for feeling stuck. Everyone hits an impasse now and then.

- I recalibrate my thinking to be optimistic and hopeful.

- I embrace all the good life has to offer.

- The only constant is change and I am embracing the changes in my life.
- I am in the process of discovering who I am post-trauma, and all that life has to offer.
- I release what no longer serves me.
- I release the old need for approval.
- I embrace present moment awareness and pull myself out of the past while making plans for the future.
- I have the ability to identify, define and solve problems.
- I am preparing myself for opportunities that come my way.
- I embrace the little opportunities in every day.
- I am curious, ready to explore, discover, risk, and learn.
- No one knows the path I need to take better than I do.
- I am open to new experiences.
- I replace negative limiting thoughts with positive, uplifting ones.

## Quotations to Help Inspire You About the Need to Revisit and Refresh Your Thinking:

*"Instead of saying, "I'm damaged, I'm broken, I have trust issues", say, "I'm healing, I'm rediscovering myself, I'm starting over."* - Horacio Jones

*"Very little is needed to make a happy life; it is all within yourself – in your way of thinking."* - Marcus Aurelius

*"You are capable of living this new healthy life. Don't torture yourself because you've made a mistake. Forgive yourself. Love yourself. You are enough."* - Sadeqa Johnson

*"Pour on; I will endure."* - Shakespeare, King Lear

*"Changing your words, changes your mind. Changing your mind alters your energy and that is what changes your life."* - Jodi Livon

*"Thoughts are energy. A drop of water, so cool and gentle can wear away a rock with repetitive drops. We are like rocks and our affirmations are like drops of water, wearing away the stubborn blocks within us one drop at a time."* - Sabrina Kastur

## REFRESH YOUR ABILITY TO REFRAME

Another way to reboot and recalibrate your situation in order to free yourself up to move ahead is to reframe situations that distress or intimidate you. You may have noticed when reading the above affirmations that many of them reframe experiences.

Listen to the way you describe a situation and take time to figure out another way to restate or describe the situation that is less distressing or less limiting. You do not want to lie to yourself in order to create a reframe. The point is to re-articulate the situation in a way that is not negative or limiting. The ability to reframe is an essential hack for growth. A reframe creates more space to live and breathe. A reframe is an opening to other ways of perceiving and doing things.

The most common example of a reframe is turning the phrase *"the glass is half empty"* (which immediately makes us think "not enough" thoughts) to *"the glass is half full"* (which is more optimistic and reminds us of what is still available to us). Take note of thoughts that demoralize you and keep you stuck and refresh them with a larger perspective or more optimistic slant that doesn't stop you in your tracks. Refresh with a reframe.

## Quotations to Help Inspire You About the
## Need to Reframe Your Thoughts

*"From now on, I want you to practice reframing other people's negativity as a reminder of how not to be."* - T. Harv Eker

*"Our key to transforming anything lies in our ability to reframe it."* - Marianne Williamson

*"The greatest weapon against stress is our ability to choose one thought over another."* - William James

*"I have not failed. I've just found 10,000 ways that won't work."* - Thomas Edison

*"Failure is simply the opportunity to begin again, this time more intelligently."* - Henry Ford

## General Quotations to Inspire You About
## the Need to Revisit & Refresh:

*"You're not stuck. You're just committed to certain patterns of behavior because they helped you in the past. Now those behaviors have become more harmful than helpful. The reason why you can't move forward is because you keep applying an old formula to a new level in your life. Change the formula to get a different result."* - Emily Maroutian

*"Wholeness does not mean perfection: it means embracing brokenness as an integral part of life."* - Parker J. Palmer

*"Sometimes I go about in pity for myself, and all the while a great wind is bearing me across the sky."* - Ojibwa saying

*"There comes a day when you realize turning the page is the best feeling in the world because you realize there is so much more to the book than the page you were stuck on."* - Zayn Malik

*"You carry the cure within you*
*Everything that comes your way is blessed.*
*The creator gives you one more day*
*Stand on the neck of Fearful Mind.*
*Do not wait to open your heart*
*Let yourself go into the mystery.*
*Sometimes the threads have no weave*
*The price of not loving yourself is high."*

- Jim Cohn

# 12. RECONNECT, RELAX & RECEIVE

Reconnect definition: *"to connect again; to establish communications and rapport; to establish in relationship again."* Relax definition: *"to relieve from nervous tension, to make less tense or rigid; to become less intense or severe."* Merriam Webster

ONE OF THE ways abusers and cults control and trap their victims is to constantly warn them about the dangers of the 'big, bad world' beyond. They may say the world is under the control of 'the devil' and that it will seduce us into behaviors condemned by God. They often urge members to restrict association with 'worldly' people and frequent only members of the cult or family.

By the time we leave, we may have deeply digested such irrational fears about people in the 'world'. We leave habituated to exclude rather than to include (ourselves and others). While we need to create a new tribe for ourselves (especially if we are being ostracized), we have been groomed to not join in, to remain apart, to exclude ourselves.

In a cult we were told to disengage from people who did not follow the cult's beliefs and procedures. Once out, one of our tasks is to re-engage and reconnect with the very people, culture, and society we have been conditioned to condemn and exclude.

We have to come to terms with the fact we were lied to, and that we developed certain fears, assumptions, aversions and patterns of behavior due to those lies. We must come to terms as well with the fact that we now have to work toward a different relationship with the world – one of being more open, accepting and inclusive. This is essential if we want to get unstuck and move forward with life.

Almost everything happens in relation to things learned from interactions with other people. Other people provide new information, alternative perspectives, tips, leads, warnings away from charlatans, encouragement, invitations to meet others, challenges to try new things, etc., etc. So what can you do, starting now, to reconnect with the world and reap a multitude of benefits?

Working toward new goals (such as being inclusive rather than exclusive) requires that you step out of your comfort zone. Working towards realizing a full, free life requires you to do some things you may not have done before. We have to stretch and lean into the new life we want.

As already addressed in this book, any time humans dare to do something new, they will likely feel anxiety. Learn not to interpret this anxiety as a signal to stop. Rather, tell yourself you are about to enter into new territory and anxiety is simply alerting you to that fact. Remind yourself that you have prepared for this step and that you can do it, even while experiencing some anxiety.

Anxiety is not the enemy. Always choosing comfort and safety is the real enemy – especially if you are working to get unstuck. Again, if you want to move ahead, you have to be willing to risk, to dare, and when you do you will almost always notice a degree of accompanying anxiety. This is true for every human. You and I are no exceptions. We need to reframe any anxiety as a signal that we are about to do something new (desirable) as opposed to being a signal that we are about to do something dangerous and need to stop.

Sometimes you have to tease apart whether what you are feeling is anxiety alone or anxiety produced by the inner conflict of wanting to move into new territory while simultaneously being told by your inner critic what you are doing is dangerous or bad. Don't be conflicted. Dismiss the voice of the inner critic and if that does not calm the anxiety – tell the anxiety to back off, too. Deep cleansing breaths can help relieve anxiety.

Moving from a stuck place requires that we stretch. It requires we reach beyond where we are now. Reaching and stretching have pulling power. You are pulled into action toward your goal when you stretch beyond where you are now – and beyond any anxiety that keeps you stuck.

Standing still, doing the same things you have always done, comfortably sitting and waiting will get you nowhere. You have to be willing to move, reach, and stretch beyond former norms and deal with any anxiety that arises as you do. *"You cannot swim for new horizons until you have courage to lose sight of the shore."* - William Faulkner

Change requires action, not just information and intent. *"By actions you choose which story ... you are part of."* - Charles Eisenstein

Healing and recovery after being exploited and abused requires a focus on the self and what the self has lost. However, after recovery from trauma we have to move beyond the wounds and our grief for the life and the self we had to sacrifice. We have to have a significant change of focus – a new, outward focus on life, instead of an inward focus on self. Abraham Maslow says the ultimate healing of self is accomplished by transcending the self.

We must shift from a normal recovery/grief focus on self to a new outward focus of action and engagement with life and the world. To move ahead you will need to focus on educating yourself, reaching out to build new connections, and creating new experiences to bring a sense of competence, meaning and fulfillment.

Since these may all be new behaviors for you, there may be a tendency to resist them. You will have to make a commitment to yourself to step up to meet your potential by taking risks and to step out of the old, confining comfort zone. It is time to reconnect with many things that were previously forbidden to you – and perhaps even things that still evoke some anxiety.

Change, growth, and movement in life do not happen in isolation. We all need human connections to survive. Good people around us help us feel we belong and feel safe enough to take risks, knowing that if/when we fail we will not be abandoned. It is people in our personal milieu who will help us challenge our fears, move out of our comfort zone, help us with reality checks, and join us in celebrating life's significant moments and triumphs.

You may or may not have created a new 'tribe' for yourself after leaving the traumatic milieu. If you have not created or found new relationships you must now take the risk to reach out, connect, and nurture new friends. Life is much easier when we feel included, but we can't always wait for others to reach out and include us. We have to take the initiative and include our self. We have to begin to reach out and invite others to join us. Ask yourself:

348.   How can I serve?

349.   How can I contribute?

350.   What can I do or give?

351.   What can I do, that no one else wants to do?

352.   How can I be more inclusive?

353.   How can I make things better for others?

354.   How can I include others in some of my activities?

355.   Could I develop a relationship with someone who is also working to reboot?

356.   Could I set up a *reboot buddy* relationship? Who could I invite to join with me for mutual support, mutual feedback, mutual problem-solving to overcome any reboot obstacles?

If you are an introvert, reaching out may seem more challenging for you than others. You do not have to change your psychological make-up but even introverts need to enjoy a sense of belonging. You may have a tendency to isolate, but if you always follow that pattern, core belonging needs will go unmet and it will be much more challenging to get unstuck.

You may need to tease apart whether you are actually an introvert, or if you are stuck in an imposed pattern of isolating yourself due to previous conditioning. Even introverts (and I include myself among them) are hard-wired for connection and need attunement and active engagement with other human beings. We all need to feel seen, understood, and connected. Life becomes much easier when we feel connected, part of something – when we feel we belong.

If you have avoided taking the risks involved in reaching out to create a new community for yourself, it is much more likely you will feel stuck. Without community it will feel more like you haven't moved forward with your life as much as you expected. I have observed that much progress happens in individual lives because of the people one meets and connects with. As said, other people often pave the way in helping us reach our goals with fresh ideas, new perspectives, leads - hooking us up with opportunities, people and places that can help on our journey, and even with resources. Progress does not happen in isolation.

You must risk, reach out, step outside your comfort zone and re-connect. This is one of the best ways to get "unstuck". Community will help you personally and professionally.

While we may have found community and support in online platforms such as Instagram, Facebook, Reddit, etc., studies show focusing all our engagement and making all our connections online with social media can actually increase loneliness and depression. We have to get out and engage in that good, old-fashioned way of connecting – face-to-face.

In many abusive families or in cults, members are not encouraged to be socially conscious. Once out, we have the opportunity to contribute time, energy, resources, and skills to our community. One of the best ways to create a sense of belonging is to become socially conscious and work with others to make better communities. The need out there is monumental and there are a legion of ways to contribute, in connection with others for the benefit of others.

Our minds use new experiences with other humans to develop and grow. New experiences with other humans will expand and revitalize our perceptions and assumptions. We will see beyond self-imposed limitations by viewing what others are doing. We increase our capacity for trust and connection and we develop enhanced feelings of self-worth due to simple things like sharing, feeling heard, feeling understood, laughing with someone, having a place where we can ask for help, sharing feedback, exchanging stories, and having the privilege of helping others.

*"We do not believe in ourselves until someone reveals that deep inside us there is something valuable, worth listening to, worthy of our trust, sacred to our touch. Once we believe in ourselves, we can risk curiosity, wonder, spontaneous delight or any experience that reveals the human spirit."*- e. e. cummings, American poet/essayist

*"Oh, the comfort,*
*The inexpressible comfort*
*Of feeling safe with a person.*
*Having neither to weigh our thoughts*
*Nor words,*
*But pouring them all right out, just as they are,*
*Chaff and grain together;*
*Certain that a faithful hand*
*Will take them and sift them;*
*Keeping what is worth keeping and,*
*With the breath of kindness,*
*Blow the rest away."*

- Dinah Craik
English novelist/poet, 1826-1887

Studies about adverse childhood experiences (learn more about the effects on the brain and on one's life due to **A**dverse **C**hildhood **E**xperiences (ACE) by reading Donna Jackson Nakazawa's excellent book, "*Childhood Disrupted*") reveal that adversity, including all the control, programming, and exploitation in a coercive control environment, literally changes the brain. The good news, as we have already learned, is the brain can rewire and repair itself after adversity and trauma. Linda Graham tells us, "*The prefrontal cortex matures – and is repaired – most rapidly through interactions with other mature prefrontal cortices. The most effective way to learn resilience is by interacting with other resilient human beings.*" Healthy human interactions rewire our brains away from the damage of adverse experiences and toward the healing produced by understanding, mutual support and trust.

Please take this information to heart if you have been isolating yourself. Take the risk to reach out and connect with others – even just one other. And as mentioned, you will have to make up your mind to deal with any anxiety this brings up for you. As with anything else, the anxiety will abate the more you engage in new behaviors.

While you may have been deeply hurt by humans in your past, you still need human connections to rewire your brain away from the indoctrination, undue repression, abuse and any learned helplessness. You need to enjoy a circle of healthy, non-judgmental, supportive friends in order to move ahead and thrive. This is another essential hack to reboot your life and get unstuck.

If you are feeling stalled with regard to finding a healthy love relationship, working with all the questions and exercises in this book will help *you* become the person you would like to find. It will be much easier to find love when you aren't operating from faulty conditioning from the past. You will be much more attractive to potential partners when you are operating from your healthy, independent, authentic self. The work you do here facilitates reboots in many areas of your life.

As you begin to take risks and connect, you must be patient and compassionate with yourself when initiatives to reach out and connect do not unfold as expected. Rather than interpreting a 'failure' to connect as a setback or evidence of stuckness, look at it as more valuable information to help you recalibrate future risk-taking.

Linda Graham offers a few helpful affirmations one can use when plans to make new connections do not meet expectations:

*"To recover resilience, we can incline the mind in specific ways:*
*May I learn to stay grounded in my body when ..............................*
*May I be patient with myself as I learn to stay grounded.*
*May I remember to breathe when I get startled or upset.*
*May I focus on what's right in the moment at least as often as I do on what's wrong.*
*May I have compassion for myself when I forget all of the above."*

Other phrases you can use to reassure and calm yourself when engaging in new behaviors and/or entering new territory:

- May I be patient with myself as I take new risks.
- May I be supportive of myself as I reach out to make new connections.
- May I learn to find and honor the innate goodness in others.
- May I learn to be interested in and welcoming to others.
- May I remember to encourage others as much as I hope they will encourage me.
- May I remember to take deep cleansing breaths when experiencing anxiety.
- As I befriend others, may I continue to truly befriend myself.
- May I be safe from inner and outer harm.
- May I trust and support myself.
- May I love and accept myself whatever the circumstance.
- May I reach out and nurture new connections already made.

## Quotations to Inspire You About the Need to Risk in Order to Reconnect:

*"A ship is safe in harbor, but that's not what ships are for."* - Grace Hopper

*"The difference between try and triumph is a little "umph".* - Unknown

*"Be brave. Take risks. Nothing can substitute for experience."* - Paulo Coelho

*"Great love and great achievements involve great risks."* - Dalia Lama

*"Success is not final. Failure is not fatal. It's the courage to continue that counts."* - Winston Churchill

*"Empower me*
*to be a bold participant*
*rather than a timid saint in waiting*
*in the difficult ordinariness of now …*
*to find treasures of joy, of friendship, of peace,*
*hidden in the fields of the daily*
*you give me to plow."*

- Ted Loder

## TRANSFORMATIVE VALUE OF NEW EXPERIENCES

One of the main things I hope you take away from this reboot book is understanding the transformative value of new experiences — especially new experiences that involve other people. There is nothing like new experiences to help rewire your brain after trauma.

Oliver Wendell Holmes, Associate Justice of the Supreme Court of the United States from 1902 to 1932 said: *"A mind that is stretched by a new experience can never go back to its old dimensions."* Now, with all that science reveals about the brain's neuroplasticity we know just how true Holmes early-twentieth-century statement is.

Feeling stalled or stuck in your recovery from trauma could be due to not giving yourself enough new experiences to replace the old and to create new neural pathways in your brain. How can anyone realize new goals without being willing to engage in new experiences? How can anyone move forward into a meaningful life without connecting with others?

## REST, RELAXATION & RECEPTIVITY

Perhaps another new experience for you would be some long-over-due attention to your general well-being. Do you make time for exercise, rest, quiet, and relaxation? When working to reboot, reset, and eliminate the residual junk dragged along from the cult or adverse childhood circumstances, you may understandably feel stressed and exhausted. You then, perhaps, need to remove one "e" from the word reset and make one of your new experiences the simple act of rest. There is no encouragement to rest and replenish in a cult or an abusive family. It is always "*do*", "*do*", "*do*", and "*more*", "*more*", "*more*".

You may now be dealing with recovery fatigue which makes it hard to embrace new challenges and move forward with your life. It is hard work to recover from trauma and abuse. It demands tremendous energy. We've all experienced feeling like the work to recover from the after-effects of abuse, undue controls, unreasonable expectations, thwarted or dashed dreams, and exploitation is just too much. If that is the case take time to be still, relax, and rest. Pressing yourself to move forward with goals and plans when you are depleted or exhausted will not work.

We can also, however, feel a lack of energy due to our own inertia. Are you getting enough basic exercise? A walk every day will make a significant difference in your life. As well, if you walk alone without a companion to chat with (and while keeping your cell phone in your pocket), you will also give your brain bi-lateral stimulation which kick-starts creative thinking and problem-solving.

Julia Cameron, in her book "*It's Never Too late to Begin Again*" says:

"*I have learned that walking quells anxiety and allows creativity to bubble to the surface ... Saint Augustine remarked ... "It is solved by walking." The "it" can be almost anything. For many of us, walking solves the problems of daily living. Not only does it bring structure – it brings answers, too. We may walk out with a problem, but the odds are excellent that we will walk back in with a solution."*

Creative ideas and solutions can also appear when our bodies are in contact with water – such as when we are in the shower, taking a relaxing bath, floating in the tranquil waters of a lake, or silently carving a paddle through water while kayaking or canoeing.

We are not 'wasting time' when we devote time to quiet, solitary pursuits. The unconscious mind often uses solitary moments to send forth its ideas and solutions for our lives. Julia Cameron adds, *"Walking is an exercise in receptivity."* After all the inner reboot work you are doing, wouldn't it be a shame to miss a nudge from your inner knowing because you never create the conditions (like the magic of regular, solitary walks) to receive it?

Sitting quietly in nature or relaxing in, or by, calm waters are equally exercises in receptivity. We take in so much information in our desire to learn and grow and we need to find moments to be alone, quiet, open and receptive. Moments when we can actually receive the ideas our unconscious has produced in response to input and incubation. Moments of rest, renewal, aloneness, quiet, stillness, mindfulness, meditation and mindful bi-lateral stimulation (such as walking) may, surprisingly, be the most productive moments you can give yourself.

Perhaps life is not only asking you to slow down and replenish but also to gift yourself with time where you simply surrender to each moment as it is – to rest in the beauty of the moment with no expectations, no demands and no resistance. Surrender to the restorative benefits of no demands, no distractions, no expectations, no noise, no obligations, no service to the agendas of others, no need to micro-manage anything.

This very state of sweet surrender sometimes magically allows what needs to happen, to happen. It is like stepping back and getting out of your own way. In a state of surrender to the natural flow available in the moment, you do not need to push or pull. You just need to honor the incredible value of letting go and letting be.

Author, Michael A. Singer says: "*All you have to do is relax and release*." It is in such simple moments of relaxation that you are most likely to receive the insights you need (although having an expectation of receiving anything would not put you in a true state of "release".). Again: *All you have to do is relax and release* ... and be receptive to, and accepting of, whatever does or does not occur. There is restorative power in simply stopping, letting go and being open.

Perhaps as well as rest, serious physical self-care is in order. If you think that is the case for you – take the pressure off. Dedicate time to take care of your health and rebuild your stores of energy. Sometimes a computer does not need to be professionally rebooted, it simply needs to be turned off for a while. Just turning it off allows it to refresh and reboot on its own. Perhaps you just need to totally unplug for a while and allow an internal reboot to happen.

> *You have permission to REST.*
> *You are not responsible for fixing everything that is broken.*
> *You do not have to try and make everyone happy.*
> *For now, take time for you.*
> *It's time to REPLENISH.*

- Author Unknown

Everything seems easier and less daunting when you are relaxed. While there are many suggestions in this book and many questions upon which to reflect, you can only ever do one thing at a time. Don't get overwhelmed by all you might like to accomplish. Just breathe. RELAX into the present moment. Release all that is not you. Begin where you are. Do what you can. No hurry. No worry. You do not have to tackle all of the questions in this book or execute all the suggested life hacks at once. Be gentle with yourself. Take it slow. Explore one life hack at a time. The projects and questions you don't get to now, will wait.

As former victims of exploitative abuse, we should be celebrating each moment of freedom secured for ourselves. Each step on the road to recovery or on the road to rebooting our movement forward in life can be enjoyable if we recall what we would be doing or how we would be feeling right now if we were still in the coercive control situation.

Take a moment to reflect upon, appreciate, and thereby integrate this entire process of rebooting and refreshing your life. Make affirming lists of the:

1. ideas harvested
2. fresh perspectives gained
3. ways dignity has been restored
4. freedoms recovered
5. plans made
6. goals achieved
7. breakthroughs and accomplishments
8. peace of mind restored
9. joys of life reclaimed
10. ways confidence has been rekindled

Having reclaimed and owned your right to move beyond the role of victim of trauma, make explicit in writing what you see as your next steps. Identify:

1. dreams you believe you can now translate into reality
2. newly percolating intentions for different areas of your life
3. things to learn, resources to put in place, and new experiences to orchestrate
4. concrete next steps
5. how you plan to celebrate getting unstuck

*~ Stand proud of your rebooted, valiant, heroic self. ~*

*"Unplugging for a while fixes computers and humans."*

- Freequill

## Quotations to Inspire You About the Need to be Open, Relaxed and Receptive:

*"Tension is who you think you should be. Relaxation is who you are."* - Chinese Proverb

*"All truly great thoughts are conceived while walking."* - Friedrich Nietzsche

*"Your calm mind is the ultimate weapon against your challenges. So relax."* - Bryant McGill

*"If there is magic on this planet, it is contained in water."* - Loren Eiseley

*"We have a choice. We can spend our whole life suffering because we can't relax with how things really are, or we can relax and embrace the open-endedness of the human situation ..."* - Pema Chodron

*"When the mind is empty and receptive, big ideas flow through every cell of our body. When we're thinking too hard, we tense up and nothing can flow through us; our energy gets stuck in our heads. Sometimes you have to take a leap of faith and trust that if you turn off your head, your feet will take you where you need to go."* - Gabrielle Roth

*"All that is important comes in quietness and waiting."* - Patrick Lindsay

*"Take rest; a field that has rested gives a bountiful crop."* - Ovid

# RECOMMENDED RESOURCES

## Recommended Reading:

Arden, John B., 2010, *Rewire Your Brain: Think Your Way to a Better Life*

Blake, Jenny, 2016, *Pivot: The Only Move That Matters is Your Next One*

Brach, Tara, 2016, *True Refuge: Finding Peace and Freedom in Your Own Awakened Heart*

Brown, Brené, 2017, *Braving the Wilderness: The Quest for True Belonging and the Courage to Stand Alone*

Brown, Brené, 2015, *Rising Strong: How the Ability to Reset Transforms the Way We Live, Love, Parent and Lead*

Butler, Timothy, 2007, *Getting Unstuck: A Guide to Discovering Your Next Career Path*

Byron Katie, 2008, *Who Would You Be Without Your Story?*

Cameron, Julia, and Emma Lively, 2016, *It's Never Too Late to Begin Again*

Chodron, Pema, 2016, *When Things Fall Apart: Heart Advice for Difficult Times* (20th Anniversary Edition)

Chodron, Pema, 2013, *Living Beautifully with Uncertainty and Change*

Doidge, Norman, M.D., 2016,

Doyle, Glennon, 2020, *Untamed*

Eisenstein, Charles, 2013, *The More Beautiful World Our Hearts Know is Possible*

Goleman, Daniel, 2007, *Social Intelligence: The New Science of Human Relationships*

Graham, Linda, MFT, 2013, *Bouncing Back: Rewiring Your Brain for Maximum Resilience and Well-Being*

Grosz, Stephen, 2014, *The Examined Life: How We Lose and Find Ourselves*

Hanson, Rick, 2013, *Hardwiring Happiness: The New Brain Science of Contentment, Calm, and Confidence*

Hanson, Rick and Hanson, Forrest, 2018, *Resilient: How to Grow an Unshakable Core of Calm, Strength, and Happiness*

Hollis, James, 2006, *Finding Meaning in the Second Half of Life: How to Finally, Really Grow Up*

Hollis, James, 2009, *What Matters Most: Living a More Considered Life*

Hollis, James, Ph.D., 2018, *Living an Examined Life: Wisdom for the Second Half of the Journey*

Jackson Nakazawa, Donna, 2016, *Childhood Disrupted: How Your Biography Becomes Your Biology, and How You Can Heal*

King, Patrick, 2017, *Improve Your People Skills: Build and Manage Relationships, Communicate Effectively, Understand Others*

Malchiodi, Cathy A., 2020, *Trauma and Expressive Arts Therapy: Brain, Body, and Imagination in the Healing Process*

Malchiodi, Cathy A., 2006, *Art Therapy Sourcebook*

Manson, Mark, 2016, *The Subtle Art of Not Giving a F\*ck: A Counterintuitive Approach to Living a Good Life*

Merzenich, Michael, Dr., 2013, *Soft-Wired: How the New Science of Brain Plasticity Can Change Your Life*

O'Donohue, John, 2005, *Beauty: The Invisible Embrace*

Pennebaker, James W., 2016, *Opening Up by Writing It Down, Third Edition: How Expressive Writing Improves Health and Eases Emotional Pain*

Porges, Stephen W., 2017, *The Pocket Guide to the Polyvagal Theory: The Transformative Power of Feeling Safe*

Rendon, Jim, 2015, *Upside: The New Science of Post-Traumatic Growth*

Rosenberg, Stanley, 2017, *Accessing the Healing Power of the Vagus Nerve: Self-Help Exercises for Anxiety, Depression, Trauma, and Autism*

Salmansohn, Karen, *Bounce Back!: How to Thrive in the Face of Adversity, 2008*

Schwartz, Richard C. and Sweezy, Martha, 2019 *Internal Family Systems Therapy, Second Edition*

Sher, Barbara and Annie Gottlieb, 2003, *Wishcraft: How to Get What You Really Want*

Soosalu, Grant and Oka, Marvin, 2012, *mBraining: Using Your Multiple Brains to do Cool Stuff*

Tolle, Eckhart, 2008, *A New Earth: Awakening to Your Life's Purpose*

Whyte, David, 2003, *Everything is Waiting for You*

Yalom, Irvin D., 2019, *Becoming Myself: A Psychiatrist's Memoir*

Zieman, Bonnie, 2016, *The Challenge to Heal*

Zieman, Bonnie, 2018, *Shunned: A Survival Guide*

# RECOMMENDED VIDEOS:

**Reboot After Recovery from Trauma Resources:**
Manifesto Template, Manifestos, Flow Chart Diagram
Guidelines for art therapy journals and/or junk journals
Decorated and lined pages as digital printable download
https://www.bonniezieman.com

**Jason Stephenson YouTube Guided Meditations:**
Guided Meditation for Anxiety & Stress, Beginning Meditation  https://www.youtube.com/watch?v=6vO1wPAmiMQ

Forgiveness Guided Meditation: Forgive Others, Forgive Yourself
https://www.youtube.com/watch?v=Ca8tAjaKhLM

**Psychologist & Meditation Teacher, Tara Brach – YouTube:**

Freedom in the Midst of Difficulty
https://www.youtube.com/watch?v=FGgklkfSYUk

Healing Self Doubt
https://www.youtube.com/watch?v=g9qMlVUxUaA

**Existential Psychotherapist & Author, Emmy van Deurzen – YouTube:**
Fears and how to go beyond them
https://www.youtube.com/watch?v=6oVqb0U3iTc

Loving your life
https://www.youtube.com/watch?v=uJgD7bDWxKs

Suicidal? Take pause for thought
https://www.youtube.com/watch?v=_IW4pyba3DE&t=38s

**EFT -Tapping with Brad Yates – YouTube:**

You'll Be Okay (Fear that things are out of your control)
https://www.youtube.com/watch?v=wP70Et2d3Lw

Not Feeling Nurtured or Supported
https://www.youtube.com/watch?v=-0swIGsUnjg

**The Vagus Nerve to Help Heal & Calm:**

Unlocking the Power of the Vagus Nerve:
https://www.youtube.com/watch?v=ZVbZOeqqwE0

How to Heal the Vagus Nerve to Heal Your Mind & Body:
https://www.youtube.com/watch?v=xPQBKe_Phx0&t=120s

Dr. Dacher Keltner on the Vagus Nerve:
https://www.youtube.com/watch?v=5d6e_Un6dv8

# APPENDIX

**Chapter 7, "RE-EDUCATE & REWIRE"**
**Excerpt** from "Shunned: A Survival Guide" (Chapter 4, pages 33-53)

### THIS CIRCUIT OF THE NERVOUS SYSTEM CAN HELP YOU SURVIVE ...

**With the Use of Simple Interventions, Your Nervous System is Able to Reset Itself**

Learning how to interrupt the brain's chronic stance of emergency stimulus and reaction, with simple interventions, can reset the nervous system and bring relief and healing. This is exciting news for those of us whose brains have had to constantly react to adversity, control, deception, threat, exclusion, shunning, and abuse.

Scientists now know that given the right circumstances and with the use of basic interventions, the nervous system is able to reset itself. It is able to reclaim neural circuitry hijacked due to the effects of trauma, and lessen – even eliminate – physiological, psychological, emotional and/or behavioral damage.

This is good news for those of us who have struggled to exit a controlling group and who are now being punished by shunning for so doing. For example, by simply orchestrating enjoyable experiences for yourself, you retrain your brain and nervous system and strengthen positive neural pathways – actually changing the structure of your brain for the better. What a great excuse to take a break from agonizing about being shunned and schedule some fun!

Many of the recommendations that follow in this survival guidebook are designed to retrain your brain and nervous system away from a fight, flight, or freeze stance toward life. As you use them, you will be using the neuroplasticity of your brain to move away from repeatedly feeling the effects of rejection and shunning, toward being more able to embrace and enjoy life. You will actually be creating new neural pathways that are not stuck reacting to feeling unsafe in the world because of feelings of fear and shame.

Let's examine one little known aspect of the nervous system that responds to simple self-initiated interventions and that can lessen our anxiety and turmoil when being shunned – the ventral vagus nerve.

You have an amazing survival and calming resource that you may not be aware of – yet. It is the multi-faceted ventral vagus nerve of the autonomic nervous system.

This section of your shunning survival guide will alert you to the power of simple interventions with the ventral vagus nerve to help you cope with the trauma of rejection, shunning and social isolation. First, a quick primer which you need to read to understand and use many of the self-help interventions that follow.

The body's nervous system is comprised of the brain, the brainstem, the cranial nerves, the spinal cord, the spinal nerves and the enteric nerves – all of which act in tandem to ensure our survival.

In the last twenty years scientists have discovered that what we thought we knew about the autonomic nervous system in the human body, was incomplete – and to a degree, inaccurate. In the past we were taught about only two branches of the autonomic nervous system:

1.    the sympathetic nervous system which was said to help us to prepare and adapt to threats to our survival by causing the body to go into a *fight, flight or freeze state*; and

2.    the parasympathetic nervous system which after the threat had passed, they said, brought us back into a *rest, restore, calm state*.

Psychiatrist and scientist Dr. Stephen Porges, Distinguished University Scientist of the Kinsey Institute has written about newly discovered or newly understood circuits of nerves in the autonomic nervous system. Understanding how these newly-described circuits of the nervous system work to ensure our survival offers invaluable help with recovery from any form of trauma – including the trauma of shunning.

Dr. Porges' research shows the autonomic nervous system is divided into three branches rather than just two, as previously thought:

the ventral branch of the vagus nerve

the dorsal branch of the vagus nerve

the spinal sympathetic chain system

These three circuits of the nervous system are connected to our emotional state – and our emotional states drive our behaviors especially during times of crisis.

For the purposes of this book about surviving when being shunned, what you need to know about each of these three circuits of the nervous system is described here:

The Spinal Sympathetic Chain (*mobilization* in order to fight or flee)

Branches of this chain of nerves go to the skin, muscles, ligaments, connective tissue and many of our internal organs – branching off from the spine. The survival stress response of the spinal sympathetic chain produces *a mobilization response*, activating resources of the entire body when it feels threatened or senses danger. The Spinal Sympathetic Chain adjusts the dynamics in every body function that can help us fight to survive or take flight to survive. It manages the fight/flight response.

The Dorsal Branch of the Vagus Nerve (*immobilization* in order to freeze or shutdown)

This branch of nerves reach down from the brainstem to organs below the diaphragm, such as the stomach, liver, small intestine, and parts of the colon – among others. When the nervous system senses a threat to survival and senses that the fight or flight response may not be adequate to keep us alive, it goes a step further and initiates *an immobilization response* – often called the freeze response. This response is designed to conserve energies and can produce feelings of helplessness, hopelessness, withdrawal, and dissociation. If dorsal vagal activity becomes chronic, the person may experience depressive symptoms along with symptoms already mentioned. Many who find themselves stalled in a dorsal vagal state of immobilization also experience mysterious physical pains moving around the body, foggy thinking, and difficulty following through on goals and intentions.

The Ventral Branch of the Vagus Nerve (*restoration* of calm and social engagement)

This branch of nerves (sometimes referred to as the *social engagement circuit*) moves from the brain stem through the face, ears, throat, and neck, down to the heart, lungs and diaphragm. Connected to organs in the chest, it is vitally linked to the breath. These ventral vagal nerve fibers are designed to help the body *return to a state of homeostasis and calm* after either of the other circuits have mobilized or immobilized the body in order to ensure survival. The ventral vagus nerve can actually down-regulate the spinal sympathetic chain and the dorsal vagus nerve. The ventral vagus nerve is essential to our physical, emotional and psychological health.

The ventral branch of the vagus nerve evolved in order to down-regulate and contain the fight/flight response or the freeze/immobilization response of the other branches of the nervous system. While these self-protective, defensive responses (mobilization and immobilization) are vital in times of threat or danger, they are not states from which one can healthfully maintain one's life.

Since the trauma of rejection from community and the shame of shunning will probably be on-going, you may, despite your best efforts, find yourself stuck in a fight, flight or freeze response. You need to know how to activate the calming and restorative response of the ventral vagus nerve. Twenty simple self-help strategies to do so are coming up in a few pages. But first you need to know about how your safety is threatened due to being rejected and shunned. *"When we are threatened or in danger ... our autonomic nervous system shuts down the activity of the ventral branch of the vagus nerve and regresses to an earlier, more primitive evolutionary response of either spinal sympathetic activity (flight/fight) or depressive behavior (withdrawal)."*

## The Importance of a Sense of Safety

The most important thing to your entire autonomic nervous system is a sense of safety – the assurance that the life of its host (you) is not at risk. The adaptive trait of scanning the environs for safety evolved to ensure the survival of the species. However, if threats to our sense of safety are persistent, parts of our nervous system can remain on permanent alert – chronically signaling that we need to fight, run, or shutdown. This is debilitating, exhausting, and damaging to our overall health.

The nervous system uses cues from your environment (inner and outer - especially your social environment) as its measure of safety. When the circuits of the nervous system cannot detect a safe social environment or are alerted to a threat (such as being cast aside from community and losing a sense of belonging), it makes a decision to mobilize (fight, flee) or immobilize (freeze, shutdown).

Being rejected, unwanted, unwelcome, and shunned is perceived by your nervous system as a threat to your safety and survival. Based on ancient patterns for survival, the nervous system decides that without the resources community provides, your survival might be at risk. You may, therefore, find yourself in a permanent, semi-permanent, or fluctuating state of wanting to fight, flee, or freeze.

Dr. Bessel van der Kolk, M.D., speaking about people whose nervous systems have had to deal with so much stress, adversity, or threats that they end up stuck on constant alert – experiencing and preparing for threats where there really are none – tells us:

*"... the great challenge is finding ways to reset their physiology, so that their survival mechanisms stop working against them. This means helping them to respond appropriately to danger but, even more, to recover the capacity to experience safety, relaxation, and true reciprocity."*

This information about the ventral branch of the vagus nerve is provided to help you *"recover the capacity to experience safety, relaxation, and true reciprocity"*. There are simple ways we can down-regulate any unnecessary or trigger-happy mobilization or immobilization prompted by the nervous system, and ramp up the calming response of the ventral vagus nerve to help our mind/body return to an open, relaxed state – even during times of perceived threat.

Since you are now working to cope with the trauma of being cast aside and estranged from family and friends, you need to learn how you can support yourself by helping your ventral vagus nerve counteract the nervous system's alarm about safety and survival due to being shunned.

When we lose our connection to family and community and find ourselves alone, we will experience considerable anxiety, as well as grief and pain. Whether we realize it or not, the anxiety is because our sense of feeling welcome and safe in the world is threatened. The nervous system interprets shunning and aloneness as meaning we are unsafe – that our survival is at risk.

Bessel van der Kolk, adds, *"More than anything else, being able to feel safe with other people defines mental health; safe connections are fundamental to meaningful and satisfying lives."* We need to know how to intervene and calm ourselves when we unconsciously feel unsafe or anxious because our sense of belonging has been stolen.

Dr. Porges says, *"It's really quite amazing how easily our body changes state when someone disengages or engages with us."* When being rejected by family and friends due to mandated shunning, we probably have several people who have *disengaged* from us. Our nervous system is thereby cued to change into a state of fear, alert, anxiety, or defense.

Porges also informs us, *"When we are in a defensive state, then we are using metabolic resources to defend. It's not merely that we can't be creative or loving when we're scared; we can't heal."* To find relief, relaxation *and healing* when being shunned, we need easy ways to reset the defensive, inner alarms about this seeming lack of safety.

The truth is although there is a great deal of suffering that accompanies enforced ostracism, our actual physical safety and survival are not at risk – *but* our nervous system senses they are, and rallies to protect us. If the sympathetic nervous system's fight/flight or freeze defensive response becomes habituated and chronic, it may inhibit our return to social connectedness, a sense of safety, health, and well-being.

Since as shunned individuals we may not readily have access to the social connections that can help us to feel safe in the world, we have to find ways to help our nervous system feel connected and safe again by down-regulating the fight/flight/freeze responses. We need to find ways to turn off the alarm, reset the code, reassure ourselves we will not die, and once again feel safe enough to engage with life. Interventions with the ventral circuit of the vagus nerve will help us do just that.

## The Nervous System Responds to Social Engagement

Dr. Porges' research about the nervous system underscores the vital role of social engagement to down-regulate the fight/flight/freeze responses. In fact, he likes to refer to the ventral vagus nerve as the *"social engagement branch of the nervous system"*. It is the part of the nervous system that helps us to relax and be open, grounded, calm, empathic, reciprocal, compassionate, and humanely engaged.

Social engagement is expressed with facial muscles, such as: warm open eyes, expressive eyebrows and forehead, kind smile, crinkled cheeks, and compassionate intonation in the voice – all of which convey a sense of social interest to others, or when we view these facial expressions in others, a sense of safety is conveyed to us. What is amazing is that fibers from the ventral vagus nerve are literally connected to those parts of our body – face, cheeks, ears, eyes, neck, throat, etc.

These basic facial cues and physical gestures tell us (and our sentry nervous system) it is safe to approach a person – that there is no threat to our safety. Barring that, alarms kick into gear to move us into self-protective fight/flight/freeze modes of being.

It is quite sobering for those of us in the middle of being rejected and shunned to learn the highest level regulating response of the nervous system is social engagement. Social engagement is the very thing we are now being denied because of being shunned!

The removal of social connections due to being shunned is at the root of our suffering and yet we have just learned that this very process of social engagement is a major part of what we need in order to best manage the challenging feelings that accompany exclusion and isolation. It seems we are in a true catch-22!

The good news is that the ventral vagus nerve is not only stimulated by actual safe, face-to-face human connection or social engagement. There are other ways to activate the calming response of the ventral branch of the vagus nerve. Research shows just thinking about or imagining a kind, loving social connection can activate the ventral vagus nerve's calming effect.

The responses of our nervous system are not conscious or voluntary. They are automatic, visceral reactions to feeling alone, cast aside, unsafe, at risk, or cues in the environment which indicate we could be under threat. Porges says, *"Outside the realm of our conscious awareness, our nervous system is continuously evaluating risk in the environment..."* It then responds accordingly, often using the more reptilian responses of the oldest vestiges of the nervous system

– responses that put us on high-alert for signs of doom, or that shut us down in fear. Esther M. Sternberg, M. D. says,

"...if you prolong the stress, by being unable to control it or by making it too potent or long-lived, and these hormones and chemicals still continue to pump out from nerves and glands, then the same molecules that mobilized you for the short haul now debilitate you."

When caught in emergency modes of response to the shunning situation, we are not easily able to recruit the calming circuits of the ventral vagus nerve to help – *unless* we learn how to intervene at the level of this amazing nerve. That is the purpose of this chapter. How crucial to know that when we are denied access to regular sources of vital social exchange, when we feel untethered, when there is no one to welcome, include, listen to, and/or reassure us, there are ways to regulate and calm the nervous system and restore well-being.

More good news: When the vagus nerve activates its calming response, it also tends to change the way we view, think, and feel about ourselves and our issues. When our nervous system is not scanning the environment for danger and on the alert to detect more judgment or rejection, we are freed up to notice and enjoy the good things around us. Challenging situations may not feel as drastic when we are no longer in a fight, flight or freeze stance against our inner and outer environment.

Because this calming circuit of the vagus nerve links with muscles and other tissues of the head, face, throat, neck, and heart, the following twenty interventions involve mainly those areas of the body. When we feel threatened or in danger (whether there is actual danger or not), our mouth goes dry, our voice may become shrill, our respiration becomes rapid and shallow, our heart rate may increase, and our blood pressure may rise. Many of the ventral vagus nerve strategies below can help counteract those debilitating physiological reactions to perceived threats.

The following strategies to regain calm do not require you to go anywhere, hire anyone, or pay anything. They are simple and easy to do. Do the ones you select for several minutes to reap maximum benefit. Even in the midst of stressful events you can find ways to employ at least one of these strategies to down-regulate any chronic fight/flight or freeze response, regain your equilibrium, and feel safe to go about your life again. This is not a one-time fix. Since life is ever-changing

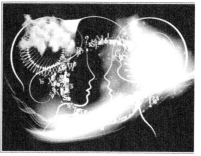

Image illustrating sensing of cues of safety or danger from the facial expressions of another.

and unpredictable, you will use these interventions with the ventral vagus nerve throughout your lifetime.

*"We get a clearer and more useful picture by differentiating between post-traumatic stress and post-traumatic shutdown. Are the patient's behaviors and symptoms a sign of sympathetic nervous system activation or of dorsal branch activity? Sympathetic chain activity results in what we usually describe as stress behaviors, while dorsal vagal activity leaves a person withdrawn and exhibiting depressive behavior."* - Stanley Rosenberg, *Accessing the Healing Power of the Vagus Nerve: Self-Help Exercise for Anxiety, Depression, Trauma, and Autism,* 2017

*"Being alive entails meeting a constant succession of challenges, threats and dangers, and regulation is an ongoing process of successfully addressing the next difficulty when it arises. We will have an easier time meeting a new challenge if we can stay grounded, do not become upset, and maintain or quickly recover a well-functioning ventral branch of the vagus nerve."* - Stanley Rosenberg

## TWENTY STRATEGIES TO ACTIVATE THE VENTRAL VAGUS NERVE

- Maintain your natural human disposition for social engagement. It is the primary vehicle to activate the calming effects of the ventral vagus nerve. When your natural inclination for social engagement is working, you are open to connection, grounded in the present moment, and empathic. However, if you are being shunned, you may be temporarily disabled in your ability to give or receive open human connection. Not to worry. There are other ways to activate the ventral vagus nerve.

- Focus on the breath, with the accent on a long, slow, smooth exhalation. Deep, slow diaphragmatic breathing activates the restorative response of the ventral branch of the vagus nerve. Take a few moments and try to reduce your breath cycles down to five or six breaths per minute. Think of how after a crisis, humans often release a long sigh – the sigh is always connected to the exhalation – and is a signal we are moving away from necessary emergency reactivity to a state of calm.

- Bring your focus to the present moment, by bringing your attention to each long, slow exhalation. The ventral vagus nerve releases its calming effects when we are grounded in the present moment.

- Let go of negative thoughts which can re-traumatize you and actually activate fight/flight responses. Negative thinking can be perceived by the nervous system as threatening, and set off defensive reactions. Positive thoughts reinforce the calming response of the ventral vagus nerve.

- Focus on present moment sensations you notice in your body – without trying to change them. *"Sensing our own bodies and staying grounded helps us to remain in a ventral vagal state."* - Stanley Rosenberg

- Activate your senses – what do you see, hear, smell, feel

- listen to uplifting music that does not trigger painful memories

- activate your sense of smell with essential oils, spices, perfumes, or incense

- touch something that pleases or soothes you

- look at things that please you in your present environment

- Splash your face with cool water. Cool water helps to reset the autonomic nervous system, and calm and restore the body/mind. If you are feeling stressed, anxious or traumatized due to the effects of shunning use this cold water technique on your face and neck often. It works!

- Use your throat and voice. Gargle, sing, hum a song, chant OM, laugh, cough, whistle, yawn, or play a wind instrument. Speak aloud affirmations to help calm you, e.g.: *"All is well. I am safe."* Norman Doidge, M.D. suggests blowing through a slightly curved tongue to make it vibrate. Experiment with Doidge's suggestion, and best to do this when alone! The calming power of the vagus nerve is stimulated by activating the tongue, voice, and muscles of the throat.

- Facial movements or expressions normally used during safe social engagement: softening of the eyes, smiling, laughing, and tipping of the head, etc. all stimulate the calming response of the ventral vagus nerve. If necessary, make these welcoming expressions and gestures to yourself while looking in the mirror. Evoke the memory of a beloved child or pet and imagine looking at them – softening your eyes and smiling in response – even though they are not actually there.

- *"Sometimes your joy is the source of your smile, but sometimes your smile can be the source of your joy."* - Thich Nhat Hanh

- Make eye contact with a sympathetic other. This does not have to be with a close friend. Eye contact with a colleague, a store clerk, a friendly glance and smile to someone passing on the street, or a greeting to a neighbor signals the nervous system that you feel safe and will help evoke the calming response of the ventral vagus nerve. If, for the moment you have no one with whom you can engage, visualize a sympathetic other with whom you make a warm connection. Imagine a friend, an animal, or an imaginary companion and make eye contact with what you imagine. Call up the memory of kind, intimate facial expressions and eye contact with a friendly other (not someone who is ostracizing you!).

- Rub your hands together until they feel energized. Gently touch and hold the following areas on your head or body:

place palms gently over both closed eyes and hold for a minute

place a hand on your forehead and the other hand over your heart, and hold

place one hand over forehead and the other at back of the head, and hold

place hands (palms or fingers) on each temple area and hold

with two or three fingers, gently trace a large, horizontal figure-eight (∞) around both eyes – the crossover point being on the bridge of the nose. Do this several times.

place hands over both ears, hold for several seconds, then gently stroke fingers downward behind the ears. Continue stroking down the neck to toward the place where the collar bones form a notch at the base of the front of the neck

*"Light stroking of the face often calms us and helps us out of a state of stress."*
- Stanley Rosenberg

- Place your thumbs in each ear, and the four fingers of each hand over your eyes and cheeks. This should be a comfortable position – make the necessary adjustments until it is. Exert pressure with your thumbs (now in the opening to your ear canal) on the little tab (the "tragus") on your ear, pushing it forward toward your nose. Hold for several seconds. This is an acupressure treatment that helps lower blood pressure and helps activate the calming response of the ventral vagus nerve.

- Massage areas of the head, face and neck connected to the ventral vagus nerve:

the back of the neck (front + sides of neck must be *gently* stroked)

inside and around rim of ears which are loaded with nerve fibers and acupuncture points

the *entire* scalp using the fingers and thumbs of both hands

- Rocking or swinging can activate the calming response of the ventral vagus nerve. Consider getting yourself a chair hammock in which you can curl up and swing, or a rocking/gliding chair.

- Go to your safe place in your mind – and enjoy the peace that floods in as a result. While in your safe place you could place both hands over your heart for additional ventral vagal nerve calming effects. Imagine smiling and making eye contact with a loving other. (See Visualization #1 in Chapter 15.)

- Meditate while imagining opening your heart to yourself; or use mindful awareness as you attend to your daily tasks. Loving-kindness meditation helps evoke a sense of social connection which also down-regulate and fight/flight or freeze responses activated by rejection and shunning. (Or use the Tonglen Meditation, Chapter 14.)

- Acupuncture/acupressure. Acupuncture or acupressure of the ear increase vagal tone – and can produce many other physiological benefits.

- Allow your mouth to become filled with saliva. Copious amounts of saliva in the mouth indicate the ventral vagus nerve is being stimulated to evoke a rest/calm response. (Conversely, when stressed and in a fight/flight response we often experience a dry mouth.) Surround the tongue with saliva and enjoy the calm that results.

- Increase intake of probiotics or fermented foods to balance the gut flora that manufacture feel good endorphins. The central nervous system (brain and spinal cord) and the enteric nervous system of the gastrointestinal tract are connected. The health of your intestinal tract and its nervous system affect brain function, mood, and behavior. Optimize your gut health and the calming functions of the nervous system connected to the gut by ingesting several strains of good, healthy bacteria found in probiotic supplements or in fermented foods.

- Move your body with brisk walking, dancing, or marching in place to upbeat music.

***

*"... in 2010 at Nepal Medical College, Kathmandu, researchers Pramanik, Pudasaini and Prajapati, demonstrated the immediate beneficial effect of Humming breath (Bhramari pranayama) on blood pressure and heart rate, both linked to the functioning of the vagus nerve. The study proved that the breathing technique, even when done for only five minutes, stimulated the vagus nerve, activating the parasympathetic system which calmed the heart rate and lowered blood pressure ... a number of yoga techniques can be effective in strengthening this vital nerve."*
- Edwina Shaw

## SWING BACK & FORTH BETWEEN OPPOSING FEELING STATES

Psychologist, Dr. Peter Levine developed a healing strategy of mentally swinging back and forth between two opposing feeling states which he calls "Pendulation". Dr. Levine says this mental exercise of purposefully moving between awareness of opposing physical states, thoughts or feelings, has many benefits which you will find below in bold text.

The instructions for pendulation are: In your mind, swing or pendulate back and forth between, for example: tension and relaxation; anxiety and calm; dread and peace; intense pain and manageable pain; – ending each swing at the side of calm and peace.

This back and forth awareness between two extremes helps the body/mind learn to tolerate difficult feelings and know there is a way beyond them. It is a way to literally rewire our brains with calm, instead of chronic activation to brace against the threat of feeling unsafe. At the very least it alerts our nervous system that there is another more neutral option than a chronic state of distress or alarm. It educates the nervous system that it can move between a state of *dysregulation/arousal* to a state of *regulation/rest* – at will.

*"Pendulation is the ebb and flow found within a range of motion. It is a gentle, rhythmic motion towards pain, the sympathetic nervous system, and away from pain the parasympathetic nervous system ... or as Peter Levine says, "... it is an ... internal rocking back and forth between these two polarities."* - Hamid Shibata Bennet, LMT

Let's apply Levine's pendulation exercise to dealing with the pain of being rejected, cut off, shunned, feeling unsafe in the world, and the resulting anxiety. Swing or pendulate between the sense of feeling disconnected, alone and unsafe *and* the sense of ease, well-being and safety you experience in your "safe space". Sit with one set of feelings for about 15 seconds and then swing over in your mind/body to the other set of feelings and stay with them for approximately 15 seconds. Back and forth several times, always ending on the side of feeling safe and calm.

Moving between the two polarities of feelings helps you to "tend and befriend" states of discomfort in body or mind. Simply sitting with them for several seconds allows you to learn more about them and discover they are perhaps not nearly as threatening as previously imagined.

**Pendulation** teaches your brain and nervous system about inner resources available that in your alarm you might not have allowed yourself to be aware of – demonstrating to your brain and nervous system that it can be responsive to your conscious choices about what you want to feel, as well as to your more reptilian, reactive brain. This swinging back and forth exercise will impart a greater sense of control over your own inner states. Do this exercise enough and you should be able to use the technique automatically when you find yourself experiencing anxiety or depression due to being shunned.

Pendulating, or swinging back and forth between two opposing body sensations or emotions, is a prime example of encouraging the neuroplasticity of the brain to reset your default stance away from a chronic fight/flight response, to a response of calm/ease. You are, thereby, rewiring neural patterns in your brain and nervous system.

What a marvelous tool for those of us who are being shamed and shunned and may feel trapped in constant terror or alarm mode. Make this back and forth technique of pendulation your own and use it frequently.

**A Few Opposing States You Can Consciously Swing Between:**

Alarm → ← Calm

Sense of Threat → ← Sense of Safety

Shame → ← Dignity

Resistance → ← Acceptance

Anxiety → ← Comfort

Isolation → ← Connection

**Chapter 11, "REVISIT & REFRESH"**
**Excerpt** from "Shunned: A Survival Guide" (Chapter 8, pages 102-110) on cognitive distortions:

### Cognitive Distortions (Stories in Your Head)
Ask yourself these questions about your stories of mistreatment and victimization:

- What are the stories in your head about being shunned?

- Do they contain interpretations which are not objective?

- Are they constant repetitions of what you have said to yourself or others before?

- Have those stories already done their work of organization and integration?

- Is it possible you are stalled in your story of disconnection?

- How do you feel when you get caught in those "stories in your head"?

- Are you perhaps re-traumatizing yourself by repeating the story again and again?

- Is there a more productive way you could be using your time and energy than rehashing the stories and reliving the pain?

- What might this current narrative keep you from seeing … doing … being?

You left the organization controlling you to begin a new chapter in your life. Once the personal narrative about what happened to you has done its job of reorganization, don't hang out in the dark cloud of the old story. Don't disturb the healing wounds by retelling old, painful stories over and over again – even to yourself. Don't tear the protective tissue off wounds by digging into stories that dredge everything up again. Those stories are from another time, place and belief system. Ask yourself if the narrative is still working in service of you healing, or if it is time to let it go. Minimize your suffering by letting go of any old "poor-me" stories in your head.

That said, we have to remember that although we have left the cult, the cult and its programming may not have entirely left us. We were psychologically coerced into buying into frightening stories of prophecies, demon possession, doomsday, destruction, sin, guilt, punishment, why people must be shunned, etc., etc. The thought reform was systematically applied and may have left us with systemic inclinations with regard to our perspective and behaviors. Much of the systemic indoctrination can be observed in these patterns of automatic thought. That is why it's imperative we observe and challenge our thinking if we want to accelerate our recovery.

Getting stuck in emotional reactions such as fear, shame, doubt, indignation, anger or resentment seem to lock one's attention on all the negative aspects of the circumstance. Once that happens it is easy for our imagination and thoughts to run wild with speculative stories about similar negative possibilities in the future. Our thoughts drive our emotions and our emotions hold sway over our behaviors. It can be of great help to examine and, where possible, release the stories in our head – especially old 'stories' we know were sourced in the cult.

Psychiatrist, Dr. David Burns says, "... *negative thoughts almost always contain gross distortions. In fact, it's your twisted thinking that is causing your unhappiness.*" Many of us, he says, are caught in "thinking traps" that obscure our vision of what is really happening and that add to our pain and distress.

**Dr. Burns' list of the 12 most common cognitive distortions (thinking traps):**

- black/white, either/or thinking
- need to be right
- always blaming others
- disqualifying possibility of the positive
- taking emotion as proof of truth
- believing others need to change for you to be happy
- selective filtering of data or info
- jumping to conclusions
- mind-reading
- labeling yourself or others
- blowing things out of proportion
- catastrophizing
- minimizing the positive
- overgeneralization
- "should" statements
- personalization (it's not all about you)

## ABOUT THE AUTHOR

 Bonnie Zieman, M.Ed., worked in private practice as a licensed psychotherapist in Montreal, Canada for over twenty years. Now semi-retired, Bonnie has authored eight books on the subject of recovery from trauma, cult abuse, and ostracism.

## ALSO BY BONNIE ZIEMAN

My Reboot Journal: *A Reboot After Recovery from Trauma* Workbook Companion, 2020

Shunned: A Survival Guide, 2018

Cracking the Cult Code for Therapists: What Every Cult Victim Wants Their Therapist to Know, 2017

The Challenge to Heal - After Leaving a High-Control Group, 2016

The Challenge to Heal Workbook & Journal: Work Out & Release Trauma Resulting from High-Control Situations, 2016

Fading Out of the JW Cult: A Memoir, 2016

Exiting the JW Cult: A Healing Handbook for Current & Former Jehovah's Witnesses, 2015

Printed in Great Britain
by Amazon